firewire
filmmaking

everything you need to know to make professional movies on the desktop

scott smith

FireWire Filmmaking

Scott Smith

Peachpit Press
1249 Eighth Street
Berkeley, CA 94710
510/524-2178
510/283-9444
510/524-2221 (fax)
Find us on the World Wide Web at: www.peachpit.com
Peachpit Press is a division of Pearson Education
Copyright © 2002 by Scott Smith

Editor: Jill Marts Lodwig
Production Coordinator: Connie Jeung-Mills
Copyeditor: Jill Simonsen
Production and Composition: David Van Ness
Indexer: Karin Arrigoni
Cover design: Mimi Heft, Zeke Zielinski
Interior design: Mimi Heft

Colophon

This book was created with QuarkXPress 4.11 and Adobe Photoshop 5.5 on a Macintosh computer. The fonts used were Cronos, Kepler, and European Pi from Adobe Systems Inc. and Letter Gothic 12 Pitch from Bitstream Inc. Final output was Computer-to-Plate on a CreoScitex Platesetter 3244 and/or Trendsetter Spectrum and it was printed on 80# Sonoma Matte at R.R. Donnelley, Roanoke Manufacturing Division, Virginia.

ISBN 0-201-74163-6

9 8 7 6 5 4 3 2 1

Printed and bound in the United States of America

This book is dedicated to the Battisti family—Brian, Kim, Lauren, and Joseph—who have provided unwavering support and encouragement throughout my challenging career. My gratitude is as deep as my love for them all.

ACKNOWLEDGEMENTS

Many of the photographs printed in this book are still frames from movies I made over the course of a year—16 shorts in all. That's a Herculean task—and one that wouldn't have been possible without the help of a dedicated troupe of actors and craftsmen. As you can see, we had a lot of fun on the set.

My deepest appreciation goes out to these fellow moviemakers: Joel Eden, Wayne La Croix, Dan McDermott, Ryan Sleight, Jason Tsoi. Paddy Morrissey, Steve Caroompas, Steve "Mango" Loew, Judy and Alex Pullos, Tony Lathanh, Margaret Fletcher, Angelica Goebel, Bonnie Skaggs, Geri Smith, Enzo and Mario Spaccia, Mark and Eric McDonald, Tom Gough, Christopher Micheli, Geoff Davis, Adriana Trujillo, Jackson Clements, Marissa Lopez, Jon Schwartz, and especially Tony Morrissey.

I also wish to thank playwright Cathal Gallagher and all the folks at his Quo Vadis Theatre Company. From this enclave of talent came actors Rosario Chiaramonte, Joe Greenan, Leona Butler, Pat Cross, Dan O'Connell, D. Michael Kane, Karie Vaughan, and Ray Ward. Through my association with them, I met the fatherly Rick Frank, an innate character actor who died before he could see his performances immortalized on screen and in the pages of this book.

My good friend Zeke Zielinski contributed in many ways—writing, acting, shooting, editing—he even lent a hand designing the cover and snapping many of the photos herein. His assistance—along with the understanding and support of Geri Smith, Connie Fernandez, Stu McIntosh, Holly Willis, Michael Rubin, and Elizabeth Duffy—was critical throughout the writing stage.

Also, I must thank Nancy Ruenzel, Marjorie Baer, Jill Marts Lodwig, Mimi Heft, Connie Jeung-Mills and everyone at Peachpit Press, including contributors Jill Simonsen and David Van Ness, the gang at RES, all of the filmmakers who generously shared their work, the gracious Debra Eisenstadt, Dick Davies, and Matt Silverman.

TABLE OF CONTENTS

Wire of Fire

An Introduction

Last year, many of the people who used my *making iMovies* book sent letters and email asking for information beyond the scope of today's video editing software. They wanted to do more with their digital movies—they wanted to archive them on storage servers or burn them to DVD. They asked for practical advice on recording footage to portable devices and setting up FireWire-based networks for small classrooms and studios.

Unfortunately, this information is sorely missing from the traditional how-to guides and student textbooks found in the Film sections of local bookstores and libraries. And although many computer books ably tackle the menu commands and keyboard shortcuts of popular applications, few address the issues entailed in integrating hardware into the production cycle.

This is a real problem because making movies on a computer involves much more than just a digital handycam and a single editing program. A DV film's success also depends on hard drives, monitors, audio devices, backup systems, and networks that carry the footage from point to point.

After spending more than five years reporting on digital film-making trends for *RES* magazine, I knew that the one aspect of desktop production which most frightened fledgling film-makers was not the software that came preloaded on their systems—heck, they *expected* that stuff to work seamlessly—but the add-ons: the hardware peripherals they purchased and attempted to install. That's when these filmmakers were suddenly hit with the high-tech terminology that sent them reeling: PCI cards, driver utilities, ID switches, termination. The confusion they felt then was enough to prevent many filmmakers from attempting more ambitious projects.

And amateurs weren't the only ones who were fearful. When I talked to leaders in the fields of DV cinematography and special effects, they also expressed concern about installing new products in their production environments. In fact, the bigger the studio, the more daunting the prospect of integrating new equipment—never mind that these studios had extremely experienced, computer-savvy technicians at their beck and call.

With the introduction FireWire technology, however, much of this confusion dissipated. Suddenly, there was greater harmony between video stream and operating system, operating system and processor, and processor and other devices. It was immediately apparent that FireWire would enable legions of aspiring directors to instantly and easily incorporate myriad peripherals into their moviemaking processes.

Why FireWire Is So Hot

If you thought FireWire was merely a thin-cable technology that connected camcorders to computers, you're in for a big surprise. Already, more than 1,000 devices can be connected via FireWire—computers, laptops, video decks, still cameras, audio mixers, hubs, removable drives, DAT recorders, and CD/DVD writers—to both professional and consumer-level workstations. According to industry estimates, more than 200 million FireWire-equipped products will have shipped by 2003.

If you picked up this book, you probably already know that FireWire is emerging as a buzzword in video circles. Many of today's computer purchasers understand that FireWire (referred to as iLink in some products) is included in their systems to help them make movies. And you probably heard salesman refer to the technology when you were shopping for digital camcorders. But what precisely does FireWire mean? What are its core attributes—the reason so many manufacturers are rushing to release FireWire products?

Among the fastest interfaces ever developed, FireWire is a cross-platform industry standard (officially called IEEE 1394) for high-speed serial input/output (I/O) processes that delivers data at up to 400 Mbps. Developed at Apple Computer nearly a decade ago, FireWire was originally conceived to support digital audio signals in multimedia devices; however, it quickly evolved into a rapid transport protocol for video because of its amazing benefits—outlined briefly below:

- **It's fast.** Make that *ultrafast*. No other technology can match FireWire's sustained throughput speeds. Although FireWire currently tops out at 400 Mbps, the next generation of the technology is expected to double in speed.

- **It's flawless.** Unlike other I/O protocols, FireWire was designed to never drop data along its lines. There's zero tolerance for mistakes in transporting footage, so connections maintain a lossless digital signal at all times. This means that video files never degrade in quality during transfer—a key difference between FireWire and other technologies.

- **It's smart.** At the same time FireWire is handling a video stream, it keeps a special channel open to send instructions over its wires. This allows devices to communicate while massive files are being transferred. It also means FireWire devices can automatically assign their own configuration information, so the user never has to worry about ID jumpers, DIP switches, or terminators.

- **It's tough.** All of FireWire's moving parts are enclosed within the cabling and connectors to ensure maximum durability when devices are plugged and unplugged thousands of times over their life spans.

- **It's electric.** FireWire devices don't always require a separate power supply, because they carry electrical current over the FireWire cables themselves. FireWire peripherals are also "hot-pluggable," meaning any device can be added to the chain without turning off the computer's power.

- **It's open-minded.** FireWire is a cross-platform industry standard, which means most FireWire devices work on Windows, Mac, and Unix systems without any special configuration. FireWire devices can also be "daisy-chained" so that video cameras, scanners, and printers link together before plugging into a single port. FireWire chains can support as many as to 63 devices.

In short, FireWire technology solves nearly every headache manufacturers face when developing products for digital moviemakers: How to quickly move huge data files from high-resolution cameras into computer? How to control camcorders with on-screen buttons? How to build network storage servers capable of backing up entire catalogs of movies? The one and only answer to all of these questions is FireWire.

WHAT'S IN THIS BOOK?

How does FireWire Filmmaking differ from other desktop moviemaking or digital filmmaking processes? Simply put, it transforms the filmmaking process, providing ways of recording moving images that not even preexisting digital tools were able to facilitate in the recent past. In the coming chapters, I'll spell out these new moviemaking procedures, in the process explaining how unique applications of FireWire products and techniques have radically changed desktop production—for novices and professionals alike.

I'll also introduce you to the FireWire pioneers who are using the technology to create innovative movies. As a collaborator on independent feature films, I've had the good luck to meet many of these people and follow their progress. Over the last few years, I've found their dogged attempts to work in an all-digital environment inspirational as they buck cinematic traditions and forge new and exciting forms of self-expression. I hope the profiles sprinkled throughout this book have a similar effect on you. While only a few years ago anyone using these tools was looked upon as a fringe artist working in an "alternative" medium, today, it's clear that FireWire Filmmaking is not

(continued on page xvi)

WHO INVENTED FIREWIRE?

When I began researching this book, I requested some information from Apple Computer. The company assigned me a public relations representative who, they said, would put me in touch with the people who could best answer my questions—the first of which was, Who invented FireWire?

"Apple invented FireWire," the PR rep told me.

I scoffed. What kind of spin was this? Companies don't invent things, people do. Undoubtedly Apple owns the rights to the technology, but someone had to champion its implementation on the Macintosh platform and throughout the consumer electronics community. There had to be a trailblazer (pardon the pun) for FireWire.

Sure enough, that man was Michael D. Jonas Teener.

Although technically Apple is the legal guardian of this closely protected property, six of the eight *key* patents issued for FireWire technology cite Teener as the chief architect responsible for their advancements. In fact, when Teener left National Semiconductor in 1986 to join Apple Computer, he had already begun early efforts on a low-cost technology to connect hard drives to one another.

Working nights and weekends on his pet project, Teener became the founding chair and editor of the international standard (IEEE-1394), a blueprint for the exchange of high-bandwidth digital audio. He was also instrumental in recruiting ideas from other innovators and in expanding the ambitions of the multimedia technology to include video streaming.

By 1988, Apple had decided that Teener's work should become an official company effort, and the project known as Chef Cat (a code name lifted from the cartoon caption on Teener's favorite coffee mug) became FireWire. Suddenly, Teener was the liaison between Apple and dozens of international developers.

Given to self-deprecating humor, Teener refers to his work on data-stroke encoding and network interconnects as simply "supercool stuff." As the technical lead of the FireWire project during the years when Apple founder Steve Jobs was conspicuously absent and the company was suffering through layoffs and dozens of threatened cancellations, Teener had to fight to keep the FireWire project alive for nearly a decade.

The chief architect of FireWire, Michael Teener, holds patents for many of the key developments he spearheaded at Apple. Teener is the founding chairman of the IEEE-1394 international committee and the editor of the original technology standard.

Finally, when Jobs returned to Apple in 1996, Teener urged him to implement the technology on all Macintosh computers, signaling the computer maker's commitment to scores of electronics manufacturers and essentially kick-starting the desktop video revolution. Encouraged by the market opportunities for FireWire peripherals, Teener left Apple that year to start his own company, Zayante, in the foothills of the Santa Cruz mountains. From the outskirts of Silicon Valley, he now consults with developers hoping to implement FireWire technology into their products.

Although a relatively obscure figure to even tech-savvy locals, Teener is still well-known among the engineers of major consumer electronics corporations. In Japan, he's called "The Godfather of FireWire," and he's often recognized on the streets of Tokyo—even asked to sign autographs.

Today, Teener continues to blaze trails for FireWire. He now co-chairs the P1394b gigabit effort, the next generation of the FireWire standard, and he travels around the world showing medical suppliers and automobile manufacturers how reliable this technology could be in the application of intelligent diagnostic and testing equipment. He sees a future in which FireWire will expand well beyond the boundaries of home and office, playing a vital part in systems used in satellites, space stations, and jet engines.

"Supercool stuff," he promises.

merely a means of avoiding the expense and complexity of using celluloid but a new direction in storytelling.

While no book could attempt to detail every offering for desktop production processes, *FireWire Filmmaking* does describe some of the interesting new devices and unheralded applications available to a new generation of filmmakers. In addition, the accompanying DVD demonstrates many of the ways in which FireWire has liberated movies. The sample films I selected are prime examples of projects empowered by this technology. The DVD also includes trial versions of some of the software that makes use of FireWire's unique advantages for digital movie production. Be sure to explore these resources as well as those listed as Web links on the disc. You'll also find an expanded list of links online at www.peachpit.com/books/firewire.

And if you still have questions about using FireWire technology in your projects, feel free to send an email addressed to scottsmith@peachpit.com. I'd be happy to help.

chapter one

choosing the right camera

Independent filmmakers often talk about "owning" every aspect of production—that is, having total control of a movie. These days, real ownership is a very real prospect. With much of the technology that was once the exclusive domain of Hollywood studios and TV stations now packed in affordable camcorders, almost anyone can capture professional-looking footage quickly and easily. In so doing, they can sidestep the costs and complexities that have prevented so many creative people from purchasing traditional film or video equipment.

Sidestep the costs and complexities of traditional film equipment.

If you're a first-time filmmaker, it makes sense both economically and strategically to buy a "digital" camcorder—your most direct path to making movies. After all, why venture into the antiquated world of analog signals—with its legacy of add-on devices and problematic conversions—when you can keep your production simple and pristine. In this chapter we'll compare analog and digital camcorders, as well as help you differentiate among the DV models available to consumers today.

In selecting your camera, remember to think of it as a function of your entire production cycle, not just the shooting process. Often times, your FireWire-enabled camcorder can also serve as a tape deck or converter box; thus, it's important to look beyond basic functionality to matters of resolution, connectivity, and durability. And don't assume an inexpensive, lightweight camera isn't serious enough for your project. Some tiny cameras are ideal for shooting extreme sports or live events, where mobility is more important than resolution. In fact, by removing the visceral quality of images, higher-end camcorders can actually undermine the gonzo style of some handheld footage.

Many aspiring moviemakers are savvy enough to know that the camera they select will influence their success with audio recording, capturing footage for special effects, and transferring finished projects to standards for worldwide film and television distribution.

This chapter discusses the unique characteristics of today's digital camcorders, comparing their features and formats so that you can make the best decision about this most vital piece of moviemaking equipment. If you already have a specific project in mind, you'll be able to quickly determine which models are appropriate to the style and techniques you plan to employ. If you're still trying to decide whether a digital process is the course for you, the following text should convince you that a DV camcorder can give you unprecedented control over many artistic and technical facets of your craft—in short, everything you need to "own" your movie!

WHAT MAKES DIGITAL CAMERAS 'DIGITAL'?

We could just say that what makes camcorders digital is their ability to record and store motion pictures in binary code. This alone makes digital video superior to analog video (its predecessor) in terms of sheer image quality. Digital camcorders are able to capture more than 500 lines of resolution—25 percent more than even the best consumer-grade Hi 8 or VHS models. And in the video world, more lines of resolution equals better quality.

However, camera manufacturers like Sony and Panasonic knew they'd need more than just this incremental increase in clarity to convince their consumers to toss aside their old camcorders in favor of slightly more expensive "digital video" models.

Hitachi's DZ-MV100 This camcorder is unique in that it stores digital images on rewritable DVD-RAM discs housed in the body of the camera. The DZ-MV 100 uses an optical reader that never touches the recording DVD-RAM media, thus reducing wear and tear on the disc. Instead of rewinding or fast-forwarding to access clips, you can locate footage by icons in the viewfinder, deleting or overwriting sequences at will. This one-chip camcorder records as many as two hours of video (60 minutes on each 1.46GB side of the disc) and employs FireWire interfaces for immediate transfer to your PC. The cartridge media also slips into your computer's DVD-RAM drive.

They needed a hook. Luckily for them, video camcorders and desktop PCs were already on a collision course—in fact, in FireWire there already existed a way to connect the two.

With this in mind, engineers designed a new breed of Digital Video (DV) format camcorders that facilitated footage transfer between camcorder and computer, making digital video superior not only in quality but in functionality as well.

Thus, it's fair to say that what really makes digital cameras digital is their compatibility with (and connection to) other digital devices, namely the personal computer.

DV's Distinct Advantages

Of course, there are other advantages to the DV format, which have resulted in a host of outstanding features previously unseen in camcorders:

- **Digital cameras are smaller.** Because the DV format squeezes picture signals into tiny bytes of data, the cassettes on which footage is stored are roughly one-twelfth the size of standard VHS tapes. And the camcorders themselves are shrinking too, with shoulder-mounted styles giving way to hand-held units—a huge factor in the popularity of such cameras today. (Think of the "run and gun" guerilla filmmakers who shoot footage while parachuting, skateboarding, and even bungee-jumping.)

- **Digital cameras record better images.** Not only is the horizontal line resolution greatly improved, but the overall picture quality of DV camcorders benefits from the use of intelligent sensors. These computer chips (which are buried within the camera housing) help increase overall picture quality by determining whether your shots have sufficient contrast and focus, and by instantaneously adjusting internal microsettings to reduce vibrations and flashing. The result is balanced, vibrant footage—minus the jitters, video noise, and white-hot exposures so common in analog signals.

- **Digital cameras record high-quality synchronized sound.** The DV format records audio in one 16-bit track or two 12-bit tracks to produce near CD-quality sound. Better yet, this superb audio is immediately synced to video data and is thus impervious to the much-dreaded slippage that can occur when dialog begins to drift out of time with its original footage.

- **Digital cameras offer lossless transfer and reproduction.** Digital video is actually compressed, locked, and protected inside the camcorder before it's exported to the computer (or another recording device). As a result, the data is transferred in a *lossless* kernel, which means it doesn't degrade—even after copying the original footage hundreds of times.

- **Digital cameras have FireWire ports.** More than just an ultrafast transfer protocol, FireWire also carries device configuration information along its thin cables. That means your digital camcorder is hot-pluggable—that is, computers will be able to recognize and use your camcorder the moment it's connected. You never have to worry about turning off the computer's power, rebooting, or assigning ID jumpers, DIP switches, or terminators. FireWire automatically takes care of all that, intelligently communicating between devices.

ANALOG VS. DIGITAL

Some budget-conscious filmmakers might toy with idea of saving money by using or borrowing an analog camcorder, and then simply digitizing the footage (using digital editing software). But this could end up being counter-productive, because the equipment and steps necessary to convert analog video into digital footage could add up to a greater expense than the purchase of a single camcorder. Of course, there are many scenarios in which incorporating analog footage into predominately digital projects is unavoidable, but the process of reconciling these disparate formats (as reviewed in Chapter 3) is a cumbersome and intimidating one—especially for the technical novice.

Analog and digital camcorders are similar in the way they collect images; split the beams of light into their red, green, and blue (RGB) color equivalents; and record the results onto magnetic tape. But that's where the similarities end.

An analog camcorder turns RGB color information into separate waveforms and issues a continuous track of signal patterns to the tape. On playback, however, you begin to see this method's shortcomings. To copy analog footage from one device to another (say, from a camcorder to a VCR), the waveform signature of the magnetic tape must be reproduced and amplified—something that seldom happens with any degree of precision, making results difficult to predict. Each time analog footage is reproduced, its signal patterns are weakened and its source footage degraded by noise that has infiltrated the new track during the recording process.

In addition, analog cameras remain extremely bulky because their playheads record frames of motion onto tape at relatively slow speeds. The greater the capacity (in hours) of the analog tape, the more slowly the playheads move. In short, the physical restrictions imposed by capturing analog signals to magnetic tape have prevented analog cameras from experiencing any dramatic improvements in performance or design over the past two decades.

In contrast, digital camcorders are compact and provide extraordinarily faithful reproduction—precisely because they *do not* record images

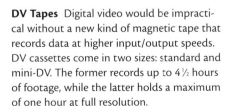

DV Tapes Digital video would be impractical without a new kind of magnetic tape that records data at higher input/output speeds. DV cassettes come in two sizes: standard and mini-DV. The former records up to 4½ hours of footage, while the latter holds a maximum of one hour at full resolution.

as signal patterns. Instead, they convert RGB color into pixel information that can be stored in the root language of computers (ones and zeros). Once the binary code is organized into neat, byte-sized packets, the data can be quickly translated to a storage medium. Most digital camcorders use magnetic tapes, mainly because they're economical; however, some record data directly into mini-hard disks or rewritable DVDs. Either way, the mechanisms that write this information are much smaller and faster than their analog counterparts.

Digital video requires a superior tape structure capable of recording massive amounts of data at high speeds: This comes in the form of DV cassettes that employ metal-evaporated, carbon-coated magnetic tape to stand up to repeated use. A special back coating further stabilizes the tape to lower noise, friction, and jitter; and a reel locking system prevents tapes from sagging during recording. Not surprisingly, these tapes last much longer than their Hi-8 or VHS counterparts—and they hold up to six times as much data.

Because they're designed to work seamlessly with small video equipment, DV cassettes include ID holes on the bottom of their housing that communicate the tape thickness and grade so that cameras can adjust their circuits to align tapes with the recording playheads. Unlike the break-off tabs on VHS cassettes, the movable tabs of DV cassettes simply slide to protect tapes from unwanted recording (and slide back when you wish to resume recording). Also unique to the DV format are cassettes that contain memory chips. You can purchase these memory-in-cassette (MIC) tapes to record customized information—for example, tables of contents, photo search hints, and camcorder or lens settings—so that critical data remains with its source footage.

How Camcorders Work

Let's face it: Most filmmakers are "big picture" people who seldom take the time to trudge through the operating minutiae of their electronic equipment. Although you don't need a comprehensive understanding of the internal workings of your camcorder, a grasp of some basic concepts can help you determine which camera is right for you. Once you understand how digital camcorders dissect colors and compress them into pixel information, you'll see how this affects lens options and filters—information you can use to compare camera features and accessories.

Capturing Color

Although capturing the beauty of the natural world as digital data is a sophisticated process, most cameras do so in the same way: When light enters a camcorder lens, it's met by a beam splitter, a prism of special filters that breaks down the spectrum into three primary colors and sends them to image sensors inside the camera. Image sensors hold thousands (and in some cases, millions) of extremely sensitive photocells. Once the filtered light strikes the surface of these photocells, its color, shade, and intensity are converted into numeric values. In the analog world, these values are expressed as signals; in the digital realm, each value is converted into binary code.

When an image is static, it's relatively easy for each photocell to get an accurate reading. However, motion pictures move very swiftly and sometimes the photocell records a blur or color smear instead. To compensate for this, digital cameras include special circuits that monitor the image sensors and survey the other photocells in order to make an educated guess about the accuracy of the pixel information. Often, a wayward pixel will be corrected by averaging the data of adjacent photocells in a process called *interpolation.*

Analog cameras, in contrast, have greater trouble guessing these in-between values, and blurred images, random sparkles, color bleeds, and noise are often the result. Because digital cameras use mathematical algorithms to examine neighboring photocells, they can compare each pixel with other pixels in the vicinity and then correct them to derive the truest color for that location. This ability to sample nearby pixels and interpolate between makes it possible for digital video to deliver sharper edges and clearer colors—i.e., a more true-to-life reproduction.

Higher-end cameras use three separate sensors to define this pixel information, delivering extremely true images but at a price: Such cameras tend to be both bulky and expensive. The most economical cameras, on the other hand, use a single image sensor to record and interpolate the three primary colors, sacrificing some clarity for a huge savings in space.

Compression

By collecting pixel information as binary code, digital footage can quickly mount up to massive quantities of data—reflected by the fact that DV tape can record 30MB per second, a rate that exceeds even supercomputers' ability to import data without serious glitches. Thus, instead of leaving all of this data in raw form, digital camcorders use a process called *compression* to reduce redundancies in pixel information and squeeze these massive files to nearly to one-tenth their original size. And all of this takes place inside the camcorder, *before* the data is recorded to tape. Naturally, some fairly sophisticated math is required to optimize data to 1/1000th of its original size without losing vital image quality.

Unlike analog video, digital video has standardized on a special codec (shorthand for *compression/decompression)* file format that protects video data during rapid transfers between camera and computer. Digital video remains wrapped and protected inside this codec, even as it sits idle on your computer hard drive, or as it's read by editing applications or playback devices. Only when you alter the individual video frames (by adding special effects or transitions in your software applications) does the data get decompressed—and then compressed again—to protect the file once changes have been applied.

Video compression is the magic that moves millions of pixels over long distances in a short time. Even after video is compressed, it still adds up to an awful lot of data. But bundled up safely in its codec, the compacted DV code can now be efficiently recorded to tape or streamed over FireWire to other recording devices.

DV Codec

THE INDUSTRY TERM CODEC REFERS TO THE PROCESS OF SQUEEZING VIDEO INFORMATION INTO A FILE FORMAT THAT CAN BE RAPIDLY TRANSFERRED BETWEEN DEVICES AND EASILY READ BY EDITING SYSTEMS. AS THE COMMON FORMAT FOR MOST DIGITAL CAMCORDERS, THE DV CODEC IS COMPATIBLE WITH NEARLY ALL COMPUTER EDITING APPLICATIONS.

Recording Digital Video

As remarkable as the tiny DV camcorders are for capturing color and compressing pixel information, they become even more amazing when you consider their efforts to write data to magnetic tape. In even the smallest camcorders, the recording mechanism rotates at a speed of 9,000 revolutions per minute (rpm). In contrast, VHS systems chug along at merely 1,500 rpm.

As tapes move through a DV camera, the recording mechanism places tiny rows of data on narrow tracks of tape. It takes roughly 10 tracks to record a single frame of video in a space the width of a human hair. Between each bit of pixel information is a tiny gap, a track with no data. These gaps instruct reading devices where one piece of data ends and another begins.

Along with the video data, there are three other types of tracks recorded onto videotape:

- **Insert and Track Information (ITI).** One track is reserved for specifying track width, track mode (SP or LP), and where video, audio, and subcode data reside on the tape.

- **Subcode.** Another track is reserved for time code, scene-index and photo-mode markers, or text data that has been superimposed in the camera.

- **Audio.** A final track contains data recorded with audio that specifies recording time and mode.

Fast as lightning, digital camcorders distill their images into numeric code, compare the individual pixel results, crunch the information into even smaller packets, wrap them into kernels of data, and shoot them out to encrypted tracks on a high-speed tape. Within microseconds, images from the natural world are forever locked in an electronic language.

The Lens

Now that you understand how camcorders reproduce color images, you can begin to appreciate how camera optics contribute: for example, the way the lens controls the reaction of light on an image sensor and how its focus either hinders or helps the semiconductors distinguish variations of darkness. Lenses are merely pieces of glass—coated with chemicals to inhibit brightness and ground or shaped in such a way as to direct light to an imaging surface. In traditional film cameras, light falls onto celluloid strips veiled with a thin emulsion. In digital cameras, images shine onto highly sensitive semiconductors.

When choosing a digital camcorder, pay particular attention to its lens because it will give you the most control over your project's outcome. In general, big lenses are better because they allow more light into the camera. However, glass quality (and the way the glass was ground in manufacturing) can affect image clarity as well.

And finally, there's zoom to consider. Most camera lenses use two pieces of glass to increase the distance between lens and imaging surface. This magnifies a camera's focal length, thus determining its zoom capabilities. On shorter lenses, the zoom range, or *magnification,* is relatively small; on longer lenses the zoom range is greater. The important thing to note here is that digital camcorders achieve zoom two ways: optically and digitally.

Optical Zoom

Optical zoom changes the size of an object in view by physically moving the glass lens inside the camcorder. A small motor wheels the lens back and forth to adjust the zoom range, and enlarge or reduce the final image that falls upon the sensor. Because smaller models cannot provide as much space between optics and surfacing area, their zoom range tends to be limited. Cameras with detachable lenses, on the other hand, generally have greater optical-zoom ranges. The maximum optical zoom that most digital cameras can achieve is 24x. The higher this number, the more flexibility you'll have when shooting.

Digital Zoom

In digital zoom, a camera's circuitry calculates how much an image needs to be expanded to achieve a specific magnification. Many camcorders boast digital-zoom features of as much as 300x. This figure is deceptive, however, because it doesn't represent the actual magnification of the image on the sensor. Because digital zooms arrive at their images through interpolation, they often magnify pictures by sacrificing resolution, causing portions of an image to appear fuzzy or pixilated. In short, the success of digital zoom depends largely on the strength of the original sensor reading. In other words, the better your camera's optics (and the better the lighting conditions, stabilization, etc.), the better your digital zoom will be.

CLEANING LENSES

REMOVING DIRT AND DUST FROM YOUR LENS IS EASY WITH A LITTLE BELLOW, SQUEEZE BLOWER, CAN OF COMPRESSED AIR, OR SOFT BRUSH MADE FOR CAMERA LENSES. WITH COMPRESSED AIR YOU CAN ALSO CLEAN THE INSIDE ELEMENT IN YOUR CAMERA'S PRISM BLOCK OR CCD SENSOR. FINGERPRINTS OR WATER SPOTS SHOULD ONLY BE BUFFED BY ROLLING A DRY CLOTH OR LENS TISSUE TO THE DIAMETER OF A PENCIL AND SWABBING THE SURFACE FROM THE CENTER OUT TO AVOID SCRATCHING THE LENS COATING. IF YOU USE LENS CLEANING FLUID, NEVER APPLY IT DIRECTLY TO A LENS; IT CAN SNEAK INTO THE CREVICES OF THE CAMERA AND DAMPEN THE INTERIOR OF THE LENS, CAUSING THE GLASS TO FOG.

Used together, optical zooms and digital zooms can produce great results. But don't be fooled by the high numbers used to describe digital zoom capabilities. When buying a camera, always aim for great lenses and the highest *optical* zoom number.

Recording Digital Audio

Over the past decade, advances in digital recording devices, compact disc players, and electronic signal processing have all had an impact on the field of sound technology. It should come as no surprise, then, that DV camcorders have taken advantage of these advances—even matching the audio quality found in today's professional digital audio tape (DAT) recorders.

Using Pulse Code Modulation (PCM) audio recording with two recording modes, the DV standard offers significantly better audio quality than analog video. In either mode—16-bit stereo for highest quality or two 12-bit stereo channels, for a total of four channels—the normal range of distortion or noise-free sound is comparable to the audio on commercially available CDs.

DV tapes allow a fixed amount of space for sound data. At the highest setting, a 16-bit soundtrack will take up all of the allotted space. However, because 12-bit audio contains substantially less data, two channels can be imprinted at this quality in the same space. The benefit of 12-bit recording is that you can use external microphones, along with the camcorder's internal microphone, to record separate channels of audio simultaneously. In post-production, you can then mix these channels at different levels to balance the soundtrack or direct audio to surround-sound speakers.

Most consumer-level camcorders include microphone input jacks that accept regular stereo miniplugs. For better results, you can purchase an XLR connector, which channels multi-track audio from a mixing board into the input jack on the camcorder. In some professional camcorders, XLR connectors are built into the camera housing for direct input of stereo microphones and mixers.

Looking for the Right Features

Although digital camcorders have removed many of the cumbersome operations associated with traditional equipment, it's still easy to get dizzy as you wade through the jargon used to describe their many features. When selecting a camcorder, keep a keen eye on the cable connections to make sure you're getting genuine FireWire ports—not a substitute interface that some salesman claims to be "as good as digital quality." Familiarize yourself with the difference in charged-coupled devices (CCDs), the electronic eyes that collect footage inside the camcorder, and pay close attention to issues of resolution, for they will affect the clarity and color of your final movie.

Inputs and Outputs

If you want to be able to convert your existing analog footage from older VHS tapes into DV format, you'll need to look for a digital camcorder that allows for analog input. A digital camcorder with audio-video input jacks allows you to convert and edit analog footage just as you would digital footage.

However, early-model DV camcorders didn't offer an analog line-in jack—they only allowed digital footage to be exported from the camera to analog VCRs or camcorders. Today, many DV cameras include analog line-in connections and allow you to convert footage easily. When shopping for a camcorder, look carefully for the Audio/Video IN/OUT labels beneath the input and output jacks to determine whether analog signals (in either direction) are welcome.

Identifying FireWire Ports

Although all digital camcorders have FireWire ports, such ports can be difficult to identify because of the way they've been labeled or implemented. For example, some manufacturers call FireWire ports by different names, such as IEEE-1394 (the official industry term) or Sony's iLink connector. And in many cases, the camera housing will use the label DV IN/OUT to designate the FireWire port.

FireWire ports come in two connector sizes: Most mini-DV cameras include the four-pin FireWire port, while industrial cameras often include a six-pin port for added durability. Since both ports serve the same function and compressed video is always protected as it travels (at equal speeds) over both ports, you don't need to worry about which type of port your camera includes.

Charge-Coupled Devices

The previous description of image sensors gives you an overview of the way color is captured on digital camcorders. The name most often given to these image sensors is a charge-coupled device, or CCD.

The CCD inside a camcorder is a silicon-imaging screen containing a grid of light-activated diodes that determine multipixel resolution. Most CCDs are measured in pixels, with DV camcorders usually offering around 300,000 to 1 million pixels per CCD.

Not surprisingly, there's a great deal of complexity buried within these CCDs. Because they collect the pixel data that determines image quality and provide the information used to monitor white balance, auto-exposure, shutter, and focus control, these chips are an integral piece of your final movie.

A camcorder's price and performance are directly correlated to the number of CCDs it uses to capture color and the size of the silicon imaging screens, or *chips*. You'll often hear these camcorders described by the number of chips they contain. Single-chip, or one-chip, cameras are usually lightweight, compact, and inexpensive, while three-chip cameras are more expensive and substantially larger in form. (Although two-chip cameras exist, nearly all consumer DV and Mini-DV cameras are sold as one- and three-chip models.)

One-Chip Camcorders

One-chip cameras store all of their color information on a single CCD, making them much less expensive than three-chip models. This also makes them extremely small and ideal for the rigors of handheld videos. What these filmmakers save in cost, however, they sacrifice in color data: These one-chip cameras must gather and interpolate all three primary colors for each pixel on the same diode at the same time.

This is not to say, however, that one-chip cameras can't produce works of substantial weight. Director Thomas Vinterberg, for example, won a prestigious Cannes Film Festival award for his DV production *The Celebration*, which was shot entirely on a single-chip Sony PC7 using the built-in microphone and auto-settings under available light.

ONE-CHIP WONDERS

If your projects tend toward guerilla-style documentaries, a smaller, less intrusive camera may be preferable. A one-chip camera is the better choice for a run-and-gun shooting style. Fortunately, advances in microprocessor technology have resulted in chips small enough to fit neatly into a variety of lipstick cameras, helmet cams, surveillance equipment, and Webcams. These tiny cameras provide footage of substantially lower resolution; however, the trade-off is the heightened sense of drama provided by scenes captured incognito by these tiny invisible eyes.

Sony DCR-PC100 This $2,000 palm-size big brother of the pioneering PC1 is a one-chip mini-DV handycam that switches from 690,000 pixels in video mode to a whopping 1.07 million pixels in still-photo mode. The PC100 stores photos on removable Memory Stick storage media.

iBot A boon to video teleconferencing and desktop moviemaking, this byte-sized video camera uses the fat-pipe potential of FireWire to send nearly full-screen video to your editing apps at cinematic frame rates. Say good-bye to clunky USB Webcams that sputter along at 12 Mbps: The tiny iBOT owes its 30 frames of uncompressed 24-bit color video to the peppy 400-Mbps data transfer speeds of FireWire, and supports as many as two of these cameras per bus simultaneously.

For movies destined for Web or CD-ROM, one-chip cameras offer more than adequate quality. If, however, you anticipate delivering your finished product to higher-definition broadcasts such as television, video projection, DVD, or film transfer, you might need the added resolution found only in three-chip cameras.

Three-Chip Camcorders

Because one-chip cameras must reconcile all color information on a single CCD, they tend to show color smearing, bleeding, and artifacting in high-contrast footage—distressing if you're used to working with a better-quality camera or higher-end format such as Digital Betacam for your shots. Three-chip cameras, in contrast, typically offer better sharpness and color fidelity, and they mix well with footage from most other video formats.

In three-chip camcorders, a beam splitter separates light into three versions of the same image and sends each RGB channel to its own chip—measuring the intensity of one color only. By capturing these disparate color designations, a three-chip camcorder has less interpolation to perform (that is, it doesn't have to make as many "guesses" about color), and true color levels become easy to reproduce on playback. Still, these additional CCDs add to a camera's cost and consume more power—the reason most three-chip camcorders aren't available in compact sizes.

Canon XL-1 This first big star of the digital filmmaking revolution still reigns among DV camcorders, and for some very good reasons: three-chip image quality, a lightweight magnesium-alloy body, manual control of focus and white balance, and (most of all) a changeable lens mount that accepts more than a dozen video lenses and extenders. Add to this an expanding catalog of accessories, and you can see why the XL1 has gained exceptionally strong critical and industry support.

DSR-PD150P This successor to Sony's popular three-chip VX1000, the PAL version of the PD150 camcorder, is treasured among digital filmmakers who hope to one day transfer their video to film stock. The DSR-PD150P provides high-quality DV acquisition at 25 frames per second (fps), making the transistion to film smoother. The DSR-PD150P also features two built-in XLR audio inputs and manual controls for changing exposure (particularly white balance), focus, audio gain, and shutter speed.

Three-chip camcorders run the gamut from low-cost consumer models to ultrapowerful workhorses designed for TV stations. The popular Canon XL-1, an affordable three-chip camera that recorded to mini-DV tapes, became a breakthrough star as soon as it was introduced and has subsequently been used for everything from simple educational videos and training films to full-blown independent features.

On the other hand, many three-chip cameras are exorbitantly priced behemoths that serve digital television (DTV) and Hollywood feature-film production. These models record their data to the higher-priced, larger-format DV tapes and host a wide selection of professional input and output ports.

High-Definition Camcorders

Make no mistake: Both one-chip and three-chip cameras offer much better resolution than typical analog equipment—and general consumers looking to create home movies, corporate training videos, or Web content will rarely need to look beyond these cameras to produce professional-looking results.

However, if you must deliver your final project for formats that meet today's television standards—particularly the greater resolutions required for high-definition (HD) broadcasts—you might consider bumping up to the quality offered by formats such as DigiBeta (Digital Betacam) and DVCPro50. Typically, these camcorders are more expensive and somewhat bulky; however, crews use them to gather footage for TV news and sporting events, which they must often integrate with archival footage originally shot on analog (BetaCam) equipment. Camcorders made for these higher-end formats always use three CCDs, and frequently feature better optics, larger image sensors, and improved data compression to collect a greater range of color information—which ultimately produces a sharper, richer picture.

Sony DSR500 This high-quality DV camcorder can acquire a 700-line resolution in a native 16:9 aspect ratio. The three-chip model features revolutionary CCD technology and digital signal processing that corrects color and image balance on the fly. This means you get professional-looking footage but can still connect to your consumer-level editing station—thanks to the inclusion of FireWire. At a cost of less than $15,000, this camera will benefit commercial directors, corporate productions, and event videographers making a transition to digital tools.

In an attempt to look more like film, some cable television programs have begun shooting episodes in "Hi-Def" with these high-definition (HD) camcorders. In addition, many documentaries and digital features are being shot with HD cameras to ease the technical difficulties of transferring video images to film stock before release to film festivals or theatrical distributors.

The major electronics manufacturers offer dozens of models of HD camcorders, with prices starting at around $15,000. Because demand for these cameras is limited to a smattering of industrial customers worldwide, their prices never seem to drop dramatically. As a result, most filmmakers prefer to rent HD equipment for the duration of their shooting, thus avoiding purchasing a pricey camcorder that could be damaged or destroyed. It's also important to note that accessories and services for HD cameras are more expensive and harder to find than consumer DV equipment. Thus, if you require a special lens or your camcorder needs repair, you may incur longer waits and bigger bills.

The Right Camera for Film Transfer

There are several other issues you must weigh when purchasing a camcorder for the purposes of film transfer. If, for example, your ultimate goal is to someday have your video projected from celluloid in a movie theater, you'll need to consider shooting your source footage at 25 frames per second, which will make for a smoother transition to the 24 frames of traditional film stock. To do this, you'll need a PAL-formatted camcorder (commonly sold in European markets) rather than a camera that shoots at the standard 30 frames per second. In addition, if you're interested in widescreen projection, there are some cameras specifically designed for capturing images in the elongated 16:9 aspect ratio. These considerations are critical to your success with video-to-film projects, so carefully examine any prospective camcorder for the appropriate features and consult a film transfer facility to see what they recommend.

Progressive-Frame Cameras

Typically, video cameras record each frame as an interlaced composite of two fields captured 1/60th of a second apart: Each field holds every other line of resolution in a single video frame. Progressive-frame camcorders, in contrast, do not skip lines when recording video; they record each frame as an entire still image, gathering the data on every line on the CCD.

Interlaced video comprises 60 fields of data per second; however, none of those fields holds all of the lines from the CCD at any single moment. By combining the lines of one field with the lines of another, the camera is able to create 30 full frames, which approximate all of the motion captured through the lens. This operation is mainly due to the rate at which television sets are able to play back video. Some manufacturers

understand, however, that videophiles may want to achieve a more cinematic effect by approaching film's standard 24-fps rate. This can be achieved by scanning 30 complete images (not half-frames) onto the CCD and duplicating each to create 60 fields. This is how progressive scan images are made.

Some camcorders feature a faux progressive-frame mode (on Canon models it's called Frame Movie mode). Instead of providing a true progressive scan, these cameras interpolate field lines to achieve a 30-fps effect—which, though impressive, actually reduces resolution slightly, presenting a problem if you intend to transfer to film someday.

True progressive-scan cameras retain all scan lines and vertical resolution for the stated shutter time, and then use this single image to form both fields of the video frame.

Television Standards

Most videographers simply shoot footage in the video format used by the television industry in their country of residence. However, if you're producing video to be viewed in countries where a different TV standard exists, you can save the time and money involved in converting your video by simply shooting in that country's format. But for matters of film transfer, there are a few other options.

NTSC

Several different video standards are used to encode signals fed to TVs or video monitors. U.S. and Japanese televisions typically use the standard established more than 50 years ago by the National Television Standards Committee (NTSC). To accommodate the TV sets manufactured and distributed in these countries, NTSC video is captured and displayed at 30 fps (technically 29.97 frames per second). Video camcorders purchased in the United States are formatted for NTSC broadcasting, which means they record footage at a rate of 30 frames per second.

PAL

French, Russian, and nearly all European televisions use a slightly higher-resolution standard, and a rate of 25 frames (or 50 fields) per second, called PAL. Because this lower frame rate is much closer to the celluloid standard, converting movies to and from the PAL format is much smoother and more realistic than converting footage from an NTSC camera. PAL broadcasts tend to flicker more like real film projections.

Recently, U.S filmmakers have begun purchasing PAL video cameras that have a progressive-frame mode so that they can record their footage at the lower frame rate—simply as a means of easing the film transfer process. When getting video images onto film, dropping a single frame of PAL video for every second of film footage is barely detectable. In contrast,

dropping six frames of NTSC video for every second of film footage results in a jarring series of jumps and blurs that look unnatural on celluloid.

Although there are many ways to deal with NTSC video-to-film transfers, more and more digital filmmakers are circumventing these technical steps by shooting in PAL.

24P

The most direct way to transfer progressive frame video to film stock is using footage captured on a 24P camera. This camera records one complete image scan for each frame of celluloid. Pioneered by Sony, and now available from several makers, this technology has the ability to record 40 minutes of HD footage on a compact $70 cassette (compared to the $400 for four minutes of 35mm motion-picture film, with processing costs). The 24-frame progressive camera provides an even higher image quality than standard HD camcorders through increased vertical resolution and the elimination of any interlace-associated aliasing.

Not surprisingly, these cameras are also extremely expensive (more than $100,000 each), and they require special lens packages available only through motion picture leasing companies like CineAlta and Panavision. For these reasons, individual filmmakers rarely own such cameras. Nonetheless, these cameras can produce footage that rivals 70mm Hollywood blockbusters, and their growing popularity (highlighted by their adoption from *Star Wars* director George Lucas and others) has made it difficult for independent operators to rent them.

Sony HDW-F900 Sony was the first company to manufacture a DV camcorder that recorded images at 24 progressive frames per second—an ideal speed for video projects that will eventually be transferred to film, because it doesn't necessitate dropping frames when converting formats.

Widescreen Mode

The CCD on most consumer-level camcorders is rectangular in shape to facilitate shooting in 4:3 aspect ratio—the most common dimension for TV screens. Despite this, some film-makers attempt to shoot their DV footage using their handy-cams' 16:9, or Widescreen, feature so that they can play back footage in letterbox format.

Unfortunately, most DV camcorders don't record 16:9 images faithfully, which means they must crop data from the images' sensors to create this widescreen look. The danger in using this effect for digital filmmaking is that the footage is signifi-cantly lower in resolution because the camcorder reduces the image sensor size by 25 percent. If you import that footage into a computer and attempt to play it back on a 16:9 moni-tor, the video must be enlarged, or "stretched," another 33 percent to display correctly—a blow-up that degrades overall picture quality.

True 16:9 Recording

Broadcast-quality HD camcorders (usually three-CCD models) employ wide imaging sensors that are substantially larger and offer a much higher pixel-per-line count than mini-DV cam-corders. Because 16:9 is the standard aspect ratio for HDTV, these high-end HD camcorders usually feature dual-mode CCD imagers, recording widescreen images without cropping and resorting to a subset of the sensor for the 4:3 ratio.

When choosing a camera for widescreen shooting, look for the phrase "native 16:9 aspect ratio," which means the CCD deliv-ers a full and dynamic range of high-performance pictures at about 1,000 pixels per line. Although these cameras often allow you to view the 16:9 footage in their viewfinders, widescreen images look squeezed without the proper monitor, making it difficult to compose shots. (Most professional monitors have a setting that you can select for 16:9 mode.)

CAMERA FEATURES

Before you settle on a camcorder, you should evaluate its optional features. Some consumer-level cameras (especially the more popular ones) have a large community of vendors who have come up with a number of innovative additions to enhance DV equipment. Often, these accessories fill in gaps by offering alternatives to the tools associated with traditional film production.

The Viewfinder

Although color viewfinders are becoming increasingly popular on consumer handycams, many models still employ black-and-white eyepieces. This is because the monochromatic monitor is favored by professional cameramen, who rely on the CRT-based depiction of video to gauge the exposure and contrast of images rather than the small LCD displays that have slowly replaced them.

If you're not used to viewing footage through a small portal, where you can see exactly what you're taping in a line-of-sight position, you can watch events with the swivel-screen color LCDs, which usually allow you to adjust your viewing angle and change settings from on-screen menus. Remember, how-ever, that LCDs use more battery power than a simple eye-piece. If you plan on using any special effects, though, you'll likely want to reference the color of each scene.

Both viewfinders and LCDs trim the edges off the actual video image as they display it in the eyepiece or flipscreen. With most videos, these edges are also cut off for display on TV sets. However, for movies that will display on CDs or the Internet, this makes for a substantial disparity. You'll need to either consider these edges in composing your shots or crop your final video clips in post-production. Either way, keep in mind that the viewfinder seldom shows you the entire picture.

Manual vs. Automatic Controls

Although most camcorders include sophisticated circuitry for managing the exposure, focus, and color balance of your video images, many filmmakers prefer to take such matters into their own hands. For this reason, many cameras (usually the more expensive models) give users manual control over these cameral presets. The most popular manual features include white balance, focus, exposure, and variable shutter speed. By using these controls with precision, you can fine-tune the look of your video, creating shocking or muted tones by forcing the camera to record footage without automatically correcting it.

Variable Shutter Speed

This feature, common on pro cameras, allows you to change the rate at which the CCD activates its line readings. By so doing, you can slow video signal patterns so that the pulsating effects of fluorescent lights, television sets, and computer screens are eliminated. You can also use this shutter control to alter the progressive scan mode of cameras, elongating the time between exposures to create a filmic stutter.

Detachable Lenses

Unlike conversion lenses (which are placed on top of existing lenses), detachable lenses can be removed from their camcorder housing and replaced with a different lens. Consumer models usually include a coupling ring that users turn to or lock in place when the camera and lens are reunited.

Professional HD cameras generally use bayonet mounts, where the lens is attached into the front of the camera and twisted to secure its place.

These lenses, which are sometimes called interchangeable lenses, come in a variety of sizes and styles. And there are hundreds of lens makers who specialize in one model or manufacturer. In some cases, lens makers can even grind custom lenses.

Nevertheless, if you feel your project requires a look that can only be captured on special lenses, you might need to get a camera with detachable lenses. Note that detachable lenses are seldom included in the price of the camera (usually one lens is provided), and the cost of additional lenses can easily exceed the price of the camera.

GET THE BEST YOU CAN AFFORD

After all this, if you're still wondering which camcorder to buy, here's our advice: Get the best camcorder you can afford and learn to work around its limitations. If you're a beginning filmmaker, a one-chip model will more than suffice for almost any project you're likely to take on. If, however, you're an experienced director whose next project may make it to a projection booth, you'll need to do a lot more homework on three-chip cameras and your requirements for film transfer. Either way, FireWire filmmaking begins with a digital camera: By acquiring footage in DV format, you'll ease the rest of your production and expand your creative possibilities in post-production.

Scott Coffey

Struggling Los Angeles actor Scott Coffey finally got to do a bit of his own casting. Approached by a production company in 1999, he was asked to direct a few Web-based shorts that ridiculed the casting agents and audition schedules most actors are forced to endure. Coffey was immediately intrigued by the idea and agreed to bring the stories in underbudget—using DV technology.

Coffey wrote and directed the 15-minute *Ellie Parker* pilot episode as a cross between reality-based television and *Ally McBeal* fantasy. The series centers on the exploits of an aspiring Australian actress (played by *Mulholland Drive* star Naomi Watts) who survives several degrading and hectic readings. He decided to shoot with a Sony DCR-PC100 and to cut the sequences in Final Cut Pro.

But *Ellie Parker* never made it to the Web—several film festivals became interested in the project first. Coffey's first-time effort was accepted by the Sundance Film Festival for its world premiere.

SHOOTING *ELLIE PARKER* WITH MINI-DV

Extreme angles helped give *Ellie Parker* a vitality not often found in debut films. Because the entire project was shot using a tiny Sony PC100 camcorder, the actors felt very comfortable with emotional outbursts or intimate revelations because the camera crew consisted of only one person—the director. The palm-size camera also allowed Coffey to swirl around the actors in a moment of panic and hold the camera just inches from their faces.

Ingeniously, the conspicuous camera becomes a central motif of *Ellie Parker*. Director Scott Coffey captured many of the scenes with hand-held shots. Here, he circles Ellie during an audition with a casting agent. As the discussion becomes rushed and confusing, the camera work reinforces the chaos by zooming in and out, and peeking over the shoulders of the actors as they deliver their lines.

Small, lightweight equipment helps immeasurably in scenes like this, where the actress is actually driving a car, fixing her make-up and putting on a performance simultaneously. The obscure positioning of the camera, just behind the rear-view mirror lends to the realism, suggesting that Ellie is driving alone. The footage may even suggest to the audience that the actress is taping her own rehearsals in the car. In this way, the handheld shots fit perfectly with the neurotic performance of actress Naomi Watts.

A small crew also helped Watts emerge herself in fantasy sequences without becoming embarrassed or self-conscious. This scene was shot with a wide angle lens to differentiate the footage from other moments in the film. Coffey used a mist filter to convey the romantic notion that Ellie sees herself in a overblown Hollywood production. This blurry, dreamlike state is contrasted by the harsh reality of the video look in other scenes.

chapter two
DV shooting tips

The fate of a movie is sealed during the shooting stage. On location, you control the set, costumes, makeup, actors, and camera movement—none of which you can alter or correct in the final footage, regardless of how technologically sophisticated your equipment is. For this reason, it's important to understand how you can enhance images before you record them.

In some cases, you must defy conventional cinematography wisdom.

This chapter doesn't attempt to address all the challenges you're likely to confront while shooting a movie—hundreds of books are available that tackle the finer points of sound shooting techniques. However, digital photography does present its own subset of shooting concerns—issues that haven't necessarily been addressed in more traditional filmmaking books. For example, DV camcorders differ dramatically from traditional film cameras in the way they perceive and record images. And while your digital equipment might offer some handy, automated features that help with focus, exposure, and color balance, there are times when you may choose to turn off these automated functions so that you can customize the look of your video images. It's these types of issues—and the way, in some cases, you must defy conventional cinematography wisdom to address them—that we're concerned with here.

Getting Superior Shots from DV Cameras

The primary goal of FireWire filmmaking is digital end-to-end production—keeping all of your movie elements in the realm of the zeros and ones. If you take steps to capture the highest possible image quality and keep your source tapes in pristine condition, your digital footage should last a lifetime. However, a good deal of your image quality can be undermined by the camcorder's built-in functionality. Although electronics manufacturers go to great lengths to give you as many creative and technical options as possible, some of your camcorder's automated features can inadvertently remove valuable pixel information. However, by being aware of the following, you should be able to prevent that from happening.

- **Digital stabilization.** Digital cameras naturally correct shaky footage through an interpolation process called *stabilization*. However, this feature can also *decrease* image quality. The best way to get stable footage is by using a steady hand or a trusty tripod. Keep your shots firm and fluid—especially during tilting and panning movement—and you'll prevent the camera's innate digital technology from overcorrecting your footage.

- **16:9 format.** Many digital cameras include a feature that records images in Hollywood-style letterboxed format—a ratio referred to as 16:9—with black bands across the top and bottom of the video footage. Unfortunately, lower-end cameras achieve this effect by clipping portions of the sensor, recording less pixel information overall. Unless your camera has "native" 16:9 high-definition capability, you should avoid using this feature.

- **Picture effects.** Today's digital cameras are able to instantly convert footage to stylized images: black and white, sepia tone, mosaic patterns, and so on. These picture effects, however, seriously alter the data of your original footage. What's more, when recorded in this mode, these effects are irreversible. If you intend to colorize or add effects to your footage, do so within computer applications designed for this use and keep your source footage clear and free of these processed effects.

- **Digital zoom.** Digital zoom changes the size of the object in view but degrades overall resolution. This is because once you exceed the range of optical zoom, the digital processor takes over and begins interpolating pixel information—a process that can be detrimental to your final footage, creating blocky and discolored scenes. To protect the clarity and resolution of your images, keep the focus and zoom within the range of the optical lens.

- **Tape speed.** Many videotape manufacturers sell tapes that extend recording time by slowing tape speed. This, too, can be detrimental to overall picture quality. To ensure the highest resolution of DV footage, always use the fastest tape speed setting, commonly referred to as standard play (SP).

Controlling the Image

A great deal of image manipulation occurs just inches from the camera—a concept you're no doubt familiar with if you're an old hand at film production. Nevertheless, a wide range of accessories are now available for digital cameras, many of which are designed to enhance pictures before they reach the imaging sensors. Remember, any changes in the optical properties of your camera will result in better overall image resolution than if those same changes were applied through interpolation or in post-processing software on a computer.

Lens Filters

Filters can be incredibly useful for changing the characteristics of light before it hits the camera's beam splitter.  Thousands of filters are marketed and sold through camera shops and video supply houses. Before you purchase a filter, make sure to feel the inside lip of your

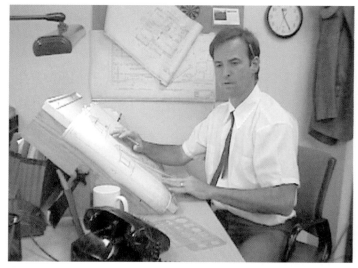

Fluorescent Filters Scenes shot under fluorescent light often appear muted (left), because of a green and blue color cast. To add warmth and correct the actors' skin tones without altering fabrics or paint colors, use a FL-D filter over the camera lens. Also, avoid shooting directly at the strobing tubes because they tend to create subtle flicker effects that can be problematic in post-production. In the photo on the right, the overhead flourescent lights of an office setting are subdued, but the flourscent lamp on the desk still gives off a cool, blue glow.

camcorder lens for threads that accept filters and conversion lens. These threads usually come in preset dimensions (52mm, 40mm, 33mm, etc.) to coincide with third-party products. The following are just a few of the more common filters:

- **Neutral-density filters.** Chances are, your camcorder already has a neutral-density (ND) coating on its lens. By supplementing this coating with addition ND filters, you can prevent harsh light from washing out subjects, particularly strong sunlit backgrounds that seem to overwhelm foreground objects or actors. There are hundreds of varieties of ND filters, and most result in a balanced exposure without affecting a scene's colors.

- **Diffusion filters.** If you want to smooth textured surfaces and wrinkled faces, use a diffusion filter. They are the staple of cinematographers who master the close-ups of aging beauty queens because they spread light across the lens without preventing the camera from focusing on the edges. Tinted diffusion filters further enhance skin tones by suppressing hard details and adding warmth and softness to images.

- **Polarizing filters.** To heighten an image's color and contrast, try using polarizing filters. These filters enhance colors in two ways: They mute the light that washes out reflective surfaces, and they saturate colors to add drama to scenes, particularly those that need areas of sky, water, and windows deepened.

- **Mist filters.** Mist filters create the halo effect so overused in motion pictures, particularly in pastoral landscapes. Unlike diffusers, mist filters (and once again, there are hundreds of types) dull the sharpness and contrast of details by highlighting object edges. Great for heightening mood, they're often used to convey a dreamlike quality.

- **UV filters.** By absorbing ultraviolet light, UV filters drastically reduce excessive blue—which means they're helpful for shooting outdoors when overcast days have removed the warm look from your scene. Many lenses are coated with a UV protection to guard against the damaging effects of dust and scratches, but you can use additional UV filters (tinted in various hues) to block harsh elements of natural light.

Conversion Lenses

Most of the lenses on DV camcorders are molded into the camera housing—that is, they cannot be removed or replaced. But if you wish to achieve a look you can't produce with your existing lens, you can employ a conversion lens. Many manufacturers and third-party suppliers make conversion lenses for the most popular cameras models. Unlike a detachable lens, a conversion lens simply fits onto your camera housing, screwing onto the threaded grooves around the outer ring of the existing lens. Once attached, a conversion lens alters the image that falls on the camera sensors. The most often used attachments are wide-angle lens converters and telephoto lens converters.

Wide-angle conversion lenses use curved glass to squeeze more image area into the camera's eye. Thus, if you're shooting video in a small room and can't back up far enough to squeeze what you want of the scene into your viewfinder, you can use a wide-angle adapter to push the camera back, creating distance between objects and lengthening the focal range.

Extremely curved wide-angle lenses will distort the environment beyond recognition, as is the case with fisheye lenses that wrap images into spherical shapes. Even with subtle use, wide-angle distortion can give your scenes an extraordinary quality, often suggesting unreal circumstances or an altered state of consciousness.

Telephoto conversion lenses, in contrast, are flat (or, in some cases, concave) and work with your existing lens to draw images closer to the camera. Frames shot with telephoto lenses often appear as though objects with great spaces between them have been suddenly stacked one on top of another. For this reason, scenes shot with telephoto lenses often appear intense or claustrophobic.

As you can see, conversion lenses provide all kinds of creative possibilities. However, beware of third-party conversion lenses not designed for use with your particular camcorder. Without taking into account the existing lens—and its focal distance to the imaging sensors—an ill-fitting or poorly produced conversion lens can result in pronounced *vignetting* (areas of darkness, distortion, and cloudiness at the edges of the

Wide-angle conversion lenses distort images to create abstract effects. A noticeable curve to vertical lines in video footage reveals the use of wide-angle lenses, and close proximity to the lens increases the distortion. Above, an actor poses several feet from the camera, and the lens gently adds a curvature to the frame. But when the actor leans toward the camera, his facial features round to grotesque extremes. Notice, also, the soft focus around the frame edges: Wide-angle lenses tend to narrow a camera's focal point, giving the center of the picture a sharpness that falls away as the image bends.

frame), *chromatic aberration* (shifts in color or shade), poor contrast, and fuzziness.

When using conversion lenses, you also need to take extra care to make sure that dust and dirt particles don't get sandwiched between lens units. Remember: Your camcorder's existing lens is built into the housing unit and thus not easily repaired or replaced.

Anamorphic Adapters

As explained in Chapter 1, inexpensive DV camcorders that don't include true 16:9 capabilities must compromise image resolution by chopping off the top and bottom of the CCD

Widescreen conversion An anamorphic adapter is a special piece of glass attached to the front of the lens which achieves the 16:9 effect optically. Several distributors sell kits for anamorphic effects, which include the necessary step-up rings, keys for mating adapter to lens, sun shades, filters, and even 16:9 LCD monitors that can be mounted to the side of the camera so that you can preview footage in its correct aspect. These low-priced adapter kits make proper widescreen video an affordable option for DV cinematographers.

imprint area. However, there is a way to use the entire sensor area on a 4:3 chip to achieve a widescreen effect—without losing vertical resolution.

An anamorphic lens adapter is a special piece of glass attached to the front of the camera to record the 16:9 effect optically. Once you mate the adapter to the threaded rings of your camera, the anamorphic lens distorts the view of a proper widescreen shot into a stretched image that falls perfectly on the plane of the 4:3 image sensor, eliminating the need for your camcorder's Widescreen effect option.

Most camcorders record footage in the 4:3 aspect ratio, resulting in a nearly square composition. This is the standard format for almost all television programming worldwide.

Camcorders with native widescreen capabilities can record images in a true 16:9 aspect ratio, a horizontal composition often seen in film production. Although high-definition (HDTV) televisions can play back this footage in its correct proportions, most broadcasters reduce this video to letterbox formats to fit in a 4:3 area.

Cameras without a native 16:9 mode must fake the widescreen effect by using a smaller area of the image sensor, reducing the overall resolution of the video signal. By using an anamorphic adapter, you can keep resolution high by optically squeezing a widescreen frame into the 4:3 area of the CCD. Anamorphic footage must then be stretched in the computer to approximate the elongated 16:9 composition.

CAMERA ACCESSORIES

Fisheye Lenses An extreme example of a wide-angle converter is the fisheye lens. Curved to a horizontal viewing angle of nearly 125 degrees, this attachment creates a high degree of barrel distortion, exaggerating the depth of scenes by pulling nearby objects closer and receding distant objects to the background. Used with lightweight digital cameras, this unique perspective often lends a sense of drama or excitement to sporting events, action shots, and point-of-view footage from surveillance equipment.

Aquatic Housings A number of companies design and manufacture water-proof aluminum housings for shooting video in undersea depths of up to 450 feet. Once you submerge a DV camera, however, you begin to lose proper light levels and experience shifts in the color spectrum. For this reason, many divers also use special aquatic lights, optics, and correction filters to increase color intensity and boost luminosity. Most water-proof camera housing features mechanical controls that help you operate the camera functions without getting moisture into your camcorder.

Transvideo Handheld Prompter The folks at TransVideo took their popular mattebox setup and replaced the heavy steel support rods with lightweight carbon equals, attached a 6-inch monitor to the front housing screws, and gave it some semireflective glass. The result is the versatile 4-pound Transvideo Handheld Prompter, ideal for crews using digital camcorders. Attached to a Canon XL-1, the entire system (monitor, prompter, and mattebox) weighs less than 13 pounds. Designed to work in full sunlight without a hood, the teleprompter allows the use of filters. The composite and VGA (60-Hz) monitor can accept signals from any laptop and flip the image left, right, and upside down—necessary to view the mirrored text in the display glass. The Transvideo monitor can also be equipped with a wireless receiver and battery pack, making the same equipment useful as a client monitor on set.

When you use this kind of adapter, however, your compositions will appear out of whack in the viewfinder—vertically smashed beyond recognition. Not surprisingly, many filmmakers find it difficult to compose scenes this way and are forced to set up an external monitor with a 16:9 viewing mode. Anamorphic adapters also limit cameras' focal lengths, particularly when zooming.

Once captured, anamorphic footage must be "unsqueezed" in post-production. The video is transferred to a computer, and easily formatted in a program like Adobe Premiere or After Effects to the correct aspect ratio. While this method does not produce true widescreen quality (it is well beneath the standards for letterboxed HD broadcasts), it does use the entire CCD of your camcorder to gather the greatest amount of data—and produce excellent results.

Taking Focus
into Your Own Hands

All digital camcorders come with automatic features that help locate their proper focal range. In most cases, a camera shoots out an infrared beam to the center of the frame and bounces it off an object, gauging its distance when the signal comes back to the camcorder and calculating how long it took the beam to return. A small motor then wheels the lens slightly forward or backward to precisely adjust picture clarity.

In matters of focus, it's best to let the camera do its job. Most camcorders include sophisticated technology for achieving maximum sharpness— automated features that are extremely reliable and generally provide the best means of consistently capturing great footage. As a rule, human attempts to counter this automation by mucking up the default settings only prevent the equipment from getting clear imagery.

Despite this sage advice, many digital camcorders offer the option of "manual" focus—the ability to disarm the infrared sensors and use the spinning dials of the lens or the push buttons of the camcorder to mechanically move the camera optics and adjust what you see through the viewfinder. The sole directive of the camera's circuitry is to keep images sharp, so you'll have to override this function if you wish to prevent the camera from automatically correcting the focus. The purpose of manual focus is to gain a degree of creative control: You may wish to soften the focus of certain scenes or change focal depth to emphasize objects in a portion of the composition.

Ideally, a camera's automatic focus will make adjustments in scenes that are indistinguishable to the human eye. However, sometimes, video footage taken with automatic focus appears to be visibly "breathing"—that is, shifting focus as the camera struggles to track objects in the scene. This subtle but annoying effect frequently appears in close-ups or stationary scenes, where the camera refuses to sit idle, instead persistently

Digital camcorders include infrared sensors that locate objects nearest to the camera and adjust the focus automatically. Here, the child's toy is picked up by the camera, which focuses sharply on the foreground element and leaves the rest of the frame blurry.

By plugging in the lens controller, all automatic functions are overridden, and the camera can be forced to stay focused on the boy in the background, leaving the toys soft and fuzzy. A lens controller can be used to slowly change the focus during a shot so that foreground subjects first appear sharp, then fade as the background becomes crisp.

searching the frame for the slightest movement (a change in the actor's expression, a fluttering drape in front of an open window) and micro-tuning the lens motor to maintain constant clarity. The result is a precision not found in film, where cameramen patiently allow actors and set movements to go uncorrected. Because this ultracrisp focus can foil a moviemakers' attempts to get a "film look" from DV footage, many directors turn off automatic focus and use manual settings instead.

The same holds true for automatic features that change white balance, exposure, and zoom speeds in DV cameras. You can restrict many of these functions to achieve more painterly characteristics in your footage, but unless you have a thorough grasp of these controls, it's best to let the camera make its preprogrammed adjustments before you slip into manual mode and fine-tune the details.

Lens Controllers

Plenty of camcorders include manual controls (focus, white balance, zoom); however, for simpler models that don't allow such controls, you can override the manual controls by purchasing a lens controller.

A lens controller plugs into your camcorder (usually via the LANC jack) and takes over the functions of variable zoom speed and manual focus. These devices, which can be used on almost any camcorder, combine a couple of features: a handy rocker for speeding or slowing changes in focus and a dial for setting the swiftness of zoom. By using these settings, you can effect subtle changes in movement, slowing the camera's natural functions to a crawl. If you need to force your camera to focus on background elements while objects in the foreground remain obscure or blurred (even moving objects), a lens controller is your best bet.

This lens controller from VariZoom disables the camera's internal circuitry to give you microcontrol over zoom and focus.

These controllers also include other useful features: They can initiate or wake a camera from standby mode, and they include a button to start and stop recording so that you don't need to touch the camera housing during delicate setups.

CONTROLLING THE SET

Beyond the lens, a moviemaker's ever-present tools are sound, light, and location. Cinema derives much of its art from the power of images enhanced by these three factors, mainly used in concert with another. But shooting digital footage requires special consideration for each aspect.

Audio Tips

Audio recording is easily the most ignored discipline in movie production—and the one that first-time directors ultimately end up fretting over in post-production. Fortunately, DV camcorders have removed many of the headaches associated with audio recording. DV audio is automatically synchronized with its video counterparts the instant it is recorded—a marvelous advance for moviemakers because it removes the complexities of recording sound independently and mixing it later.

Synchronized audio, however, is a double-edged sword: On one hand, DV audio is extremely high quality, which means it's likely to be your best source. In fact, the quality of the built-in microphones and recording levels of today's DV camcorders is entirely adequate for most shoots. On the other hand, this extremely sensitive equipment can pick up the slightest sounds on your set: the breathing of the camera operator, birds flying overhead, distant traffic, crowd murmurs. Make sure you shield your camera's built-in microphone from any disruptive noises that might prevent you from hearing the actors' dialogue. Low-frequency noises—computer hard drives, refrigerators, car engines, windy weather—are often distinct enough to be heard on DV tape but ignored by the human ear. In many cases, these sounds help create a sense of reality; however, they can also interfere with your ability to produce a cohesive soundtrack .

External Audio Accessories

To avoid unwanted noise (or simply to produce your sound effects in different ways), you can enlist the help of external or remote microphones and professional mixing equipment. Sadly, not a lot of manufacturers are rushing to supply audio accessories for digital camcorders—perhaps because most camcorders come with adequate built-in microphones. If you need professional sound quality, look for a camera that allows you to attach an external microphone.

To use a professional microphone, you'll likely need an XLR adapter, which some camera manufacturers supply or offer as optional purchases. An XLR connector (the term stands for *external, live,* and *return*) is a circular three-pin, shielded conductor commonly found in professional recording equipment for connecting low-level balanced audio signals with instruments and microphones.

High-end cameras include XLR connections on their hot shoe (a powered bay of audio plugs). However, it's important to point out that in many supplied XLR adapters, the microphone must pull its required DC power voltage from the hot

Professional Plugs An XLR adapter bridges the divide between the bulky, industrial connectors used in professional recording studios and the lightweight plugs found on most camcorders. This device conveniently includes simple level adjustments to harmoniously mix two external microphones into a single audio input source.

shoe of the camcorder itself. By using a power supply (or other equipment) with unshielded connectors or inappropriate power adapters, you may introduce additional noise.

Some filmmakers insist on a "double system" for sound recording. They capture audio from a mixing board into a DAT recorder, and also run the audio mix into the camcorder using a third-party stereo XLR adapter—sage advice for DV operators.

But be careful: Some camcorders don't cut off the built-in microphone when an external audio source is present, which means they're capturing an additional recording at the same time. As a result, you may get extra noise and an unwanted tone in your soundtrack.

Lighting

There's no real secret to setting up proper lighting for digital cameras. On most movie sets involving interior scenes, cameramen typically employ a three-light setup, where a main light source provides the brightest illumination on the subject, and two smaller light sources act as highlights for the back and sides of the same object. These smaller lights often serve to distance the subject from its background and diffuse the shadows created by the main light source. Almost all shots are composed using three simple light sources or some variation of the same.

The only difference between videotape lighting and film lighting is that digital technology records a narrower range of sensitivity, particularly in areas of extreme exposure. Digital video is unable to retain detailed color information in the brightest portions of the frame and struggles to keep the darkest areas of images flat—especially in low-light conditions. For optimum results, DV cinematographers should consider staying safely in the middle ranges of light, never shooting in high luminance or persistent darkness.

Another trouble sign for digital video is the marriage of these extremes—scenes of high contrast between glaring white and pitch black. As a rule, you should maintain exposure levels that prevent your picture elements from exceeding 80 percent of total white. This way, you allow the camera to record some color information (no matter how faint) in all pixel areas of the frame. Likewise, you shouldn't attempt to reach deep blackness in any corner of the image since such efforts will ultimately reveal speckled noise in those areas. In the absence of clearly identifiable color, the camera will infuse the pixels with interpolated information that appears static in the final footage.

Don't try to outwit the camera in a computer program by shooting blown-out whites or heavy shadows. Extreme footage produces troublesome noise, which may not appear to be

Most of today's DV camcorders do a superior job of adjusting to changes in natural light. However, when sunlight presents a bright background to your subject, you may wish to adjust the camera settings to dull its intensifying effects. Because the boy appeared too dark against the sky, this shot was brightened with exposure controls to allow his face to be seen clearly.

Adjusting the exposure controls too much, however, can cause the camera to "blow out" the brightest areas of the image. In this close-up, all color detail is missing from the background sky and portions of the boy's face. These areas, devoid of color information, contain no pixel color information and cannot be corrected in post-production. A better solution would have been to project (or reflect) sunlight onto the subject and lower the exposure settings until substantial tonality in both the sky and the boy were apparent in the image.

problematic at first but once compressed or exaggerated through software, will produce fluttering artifacts that can be distracting to the viewer.

The best policy is to shoot in strong light but lower the levels to reduce any areas of white-hot flare or overexposure. Use household lamps and position actors near windows, but don't point the camera directly toward your light source. In addition, minimize shadow sizes and limit dark areas to the edges of your compositions. Finally, wherever possible, use color to fill in large areas or to add luminance in place of a harsh light.

Sunlight

Cinematographers playfully refer to the sun as a single thermonuclear fusion-based light source conveniently placed 93 million miles from your subject. Due to this remarkable positioning, the sun provides perfect corner-to-corner illumination in most situations and makes it easy to expertly match shots from day to day. Of course, the sun can also present problems in lighting, moving frequently, casting harsh shadows, and shining relentlessly off chrome, glass, or water surfaces. Still, for quick and easy shooting, the sun is an ideal lamp, and most DV camcorders are well-equipped to adjust to its overpowering effects.

Using Reflectors and Diffusers

Although the merits of reflectors and diffusers are well known in film circles, they should be even more heralded among DV moviemakers. These great equalizers add and subtract light instantaneously without forcing your crew to route electricity or construct new supports. What's more, you can purchase them at most photography supply stores; you can even use household objects as substitutes!

Natural sunlight can also draw undue attention to a setting. Here, a late-afternoon sunset brightens up the landscape until it overwhelms the composition and diverts the viewer's attention. Subsequently, the camcorder automatically balances its exposure, darkening the foreground elements (in this case, the actors). Reflecting light onto the actors would not solve this problem—the background would still be distracting.

By waiting for the sun to set, the scene has been salvaged. Often, twilight or overcast skies produce the best conditions for outdoor shots (though they dramatically limit shooting time) and give your DV camcorder the least cause to overcorrect poor lighting situations.

Reflectors come in many shapes and sizes. When shooting in shadows, it often becomes necessary to use a reflector to redirect sunshine toward the actors. This way, your footage benefits from the pinpointing spotlight of the reflector and an even scene free of harsh shadows.

Backlit scenes often require reflectors to balance their composition. In this crowd scene, the bright circus tent in the background outshines the actors in the foreground. With reflected light aimed at their faces, the actors now appear fully exposed to the camera. The shot retains the silhouette of their actions yet picks up the detail of their expressions.

Diffusers usually comprise translucent materials designed to sit between a light source and its subject, scattering the rays to remove glare, dispense softer light over a broader space, or fill in shadow areas. Reflectors, in contrast, are generally made of opaque, metallic materials, though sheets of bright foam core or aluminum foil can easily replicate their effects. As their name suggests, reflectors bounce light and redirect it elsewhere. Usually, camera operators aim lights toward a ceiling or off walls to spread illumination over bigger areas; however, small reflectors can direct light into small areas, filling in shadows or aiming overhead lights back up into the faces of actors.

Reflectors and diffusers are vital to controlling the balance and exposure in digital cameras. They eliminate the need for additional light sources (which add heat to sets and require extra power cords and outlets), and they help keep light levels in the middle ranges, taking the hot glow out of extreme whites and giving much-needed detail to shadow areas.

Dressing Actors and Sets for DV

As with all movie shoots, it's important to pay attention to the small problems that sets and costumes can create for the camera. Shiny jewelry, slick hair, metallic fabrics, and patent leather can all reflect light into the lens. Likewise, certain hats and hairstyles may cast awkward shadows over actors' faces.

When selecting costumes for a DV production, avoid any clothing with contrasting logos, solid black or white shirts, and materials with small, repeating patterns such as checks or intricate plaids, which can distort when presented on a television screen. It's also best to avoid tightly woven patterns in your fabrics (like checkers and stripes) because they can cause a jittering effect in the video signal when a character is moving. Patterns that feature contrasting colors often appear to be vibrate, giving the impression that the costume is glowing.

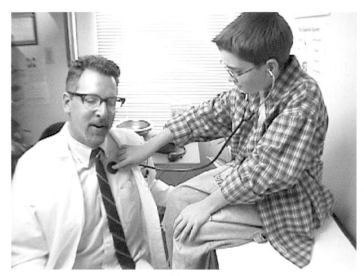

Beware of patterns in costume and set design and keep your sets clear of lines and grids that may become distorted when displayed on a television monitor. In this scene, the Venetian blinds have created a strange moiré pattern that shifts as the camera moves; the doctor's white smock flares and reflects light uncontrollably; and the boy's wrinkled and ruffled flannel shirt contains a busy print that muddles his actions.

Color saturation on digital video can also be problematic. For this reason, avoid colors that are extremely light or dark. Characters wearing white—or even off-white—shirts may reflect too much light around their faces and the faces of nearby actors. In bright conditions, elements of white clothing can become overexposed, making details such as pockets, buttons, and collars indistinguishable from the shirt. Details in dark-blue and near-black clothing are equally difficult to differentiate, even under professional camera lighting. For this reason, you should avoid situations that force actors to wear dark colors against a dark background—in many cases, their heads will appear to be floating in a sea of darkness! A good rule of thumb is to stick to varying colors of clothing in medium tones and look for optimal light in all situations.

There's no need to shy away from using candlelight or fires as light sources in your scenes, but you should take care to prevent flaring in the video. The best way to adjust for an open flame is to slightly underexpose the footage by adjusting your camera, then dapple the set with additional light to compensate for darkness. Here, a group of hobos gather around a campfire. Once the master shot has established the fire as the primary light source, the camera operator can take subsequent shots with supplemental lights. In the close-ups, the flames of the roaring fire still appear as flickering light on the outside characters, but the middle actor has been accentuated with several lights hidden behind his fellow actors.

SHOOTING FOR THE WEB

Shooting video for presentation over the Internet is radically different from standard moviemaking. Thus, you must consider several key dynamics when preparing your shot selections. The factors that determine how your movie will appear over the Web are governed by the video compression software used to squeeze your raw DV signal into downloadable or streaming files. The quality of Web-compressed video depends largely on the movement and luminance of your footage. To dramatically improve movies destined for the Web, consider these shooting tips:

- *Keep the action steady.* Reduce the amount of fast and extended motion in your movie because high-speed action sequences result in sluggish playback.

- *Use well-lit scenes.* Because dark settings present difficulties in compression, you'll want to avoid videotaping in low-light conditions.

- *Compose for contrast.* When creating compositions for the Web, contrast is more important than color because drastic compression leaves little room for color fidelity.

- *Avoid patterns.* Keep details to a minimum because they significantly inhibit the compression software from reducing the final file size of your movie. Make sure you shoot against an unchanging background.

- *Use close-ups and silhouettes.* Since long-shot compositions struggle to communicate subtle movement, shoot all vital action in close-up, or silhouette them until they become clearly distinguishable when displayed inside a small window.

- *Avoid Zooming.* Zooming in for close-up shots forces the computer to compress the entire frame rather than just subtle changes in facial features. Instead, have actors move closer to the camera, which doesn't require as much overall compression.

Because Web audiences will likely view your movie at matchbook size, vital actions will be undecipherable unless they're staged in clear view. Use plenty of close-ups for scenes involving pivotal hand gestures or important dialogue, and have your actors exaggerate their movements for purposes of clarity.

If your projects are intended for the Internet, you should also take into account the many variables that can inhibit compressing footage into streaming formats. In this close-up, an oversized rope is used to clearly communicate the situation as well as to alleviate the compression problems inherent in the intricate details of a finer weave.

Color Saturation

Simply put, color fidelity in DV footage is not as reliable as color fidelity in film. Because digital video is immediately compressed into the DV codec inside the camera, the pixel sampling that takes place tends to favor the needs of high-speed data storage at the expense of color accuracy. Two conditions arise from this shortcoming: DV cameras have difficulty handling colors that are oversaturated and, in low-light situations, these saturated areas can become very "noisy," full of pixel particles that seem to flicker constantly. Of course, the easiest way to correct color saturation is via adequate lighting. However, in many cases, you'll need to adjust the camera's gain setting to compensate for color saturation produced by strong backlighting, direct sunlight, or color noise in dark locations.

Reducing Contrast

Some videographers attempt to match the fluidity of film stock by reducing the sharp contrast inherent in the video image. As with lighting, DV cameras have a narrow range of tonal representation in the picture signal, so they tend to stay in settings of acute contrast. Wide-angle and telephoto lens converters naturally curve the lens, softening the edges of image edges, and lens filters go even further in removing the distinctions between film and video.

If you desire a more filmic look for your video footage, pay close attention to contrast effects. Use soft-contrast or fog filters to soften the sharp edges of shadows and light that affect a scene's overall look. And favor color contrast and deep, loose focus over harsh lighting whenever possible. Finally, while you're at it, turn the camera's internal menu settings for sharpness all the way down. You can apply each of these techniques without risking image clarity or resolution.

SHOOTING FOR SPECIAL EFFECTS

A considerable amount of mystery has been assigned to chromakey effects, or "green screen" shots, particularly in conjunction with consumer DV cameras. *Chromakey* refers to the process of removing a chromatic color from a frame of video to create a "key," or matte, around an object. Once a key has been established, the matted object can be easily composited with other footage to "sandwich" elements together for dramatic effects.

Although people may tell you that the relatively low luminance information of DV 4:1:1 compression is less than ideal for capturing quality footage for demanding post-production work, this rumor is completely unfounded: Digital video—even the mini-DV format—can produce rich-looking special effects on a shoestring budget. All that's required is a bit of patience, some understanding of lighting and color, and thoughtful planning before shooting scenes that will be used as matte or chromakey ("green screen") elements.

Traditionally, green and blue have been favored for this use. Since blue light complements natural skin tone and is the most sensitive to film stock emulsion, it was once the logical choice for avoiding conflicts in optical processes. Today, however, digital-camera operators prefer green chroma backgrounds because video cameras are more sensitive to that color, and chromakey applications gather better luminance and color data from multiple channels of the video signal. In addition, green is a better reflector than blue; it doesn't create as much spill color on nearby objects; and it provides greater flexibility when matting blue objects in the foreground.

Setting up chromakey shots involves some planning: This actor is filmed diagonally against a green background. After importing this footage to the computer, a software program will automatically remove all green areas of the frame (thus, you don't want your actor's costume to contain this color). Because unwanted reflections in the interlaced areas or edges of the actor's outline must be painstakingly removed, strong lighting is critical.

While photographing miniatures is often straightforward, it's important to hide as many extraneous elements as possible (in this case, the fishing wires and clamps) to reduce the amount of cleanup work required in post-production.

Lighting Chromakey Scenes

Green-screen scenes should be lit evenly so that a continuous chromatic tone is provided from which the computer can pull a successful key. The industry term for this is *flat lighting*; however, it should only refer to the background: Objects and actors in the foreground of a chromakey scene should be lit independently of the background, and their lighting should be dramatic and well-designed. Make sure to take notes about your lighting set-up during the shooting stage so that you can match separately photographed elements that will wind up sharing the same frame.

Chromakey scenes are seldom lit with much subtlety: On the one hand, it's easy to overlight them, while on the other, poorly lit chromakey scenes can require hours of cleanup to transform uneven backgrounds into workable mattes. Save yourself

Once the shots are combined, the software will adjust luminance properties to equalize differences and seamlessly integrate them. This shot was then colorized and the spraying blood was added as a paint effect.

headaches by avoiding the use of smoke, water, wispy hair, or semitransparent objects in green-screen footage.

Shadows are another matter: In many cases, you'll want to record distinct shadows to give the final composite scene a feeling of reality. These shadows, however, are difficult to produce indoors, which means you may want to film such scenes in broad daylight. Once again, record the hour of day you shoot these scenes so that you can later match the shadow cast with other objects and shoot them in similar conditions. Overall, daylight provides fantastic illumination for green-screen shots—even though setup can take longer and shadows may shift during longer shooting periods.

To capture a distinct shadow, this shot was set up outdoors in natural daylight. The sun provides excellent illumination for these shots, producing a strong, single shadow that will fall away cleanly from the color key.

Well-lit, evenly distributed color is ideal for pulling a proper key. Notice how the separation between the actor and the background prevents the green color from "spilling," or reflecting, onto the actor's costume or props.

Poor chromakey lighting can equal hours of cleanup. This shot contains too many wrinkles, folds, shadows, and hot spots to pull an even key. Note the lens flare created by the exposed light bulb. The result will be an unusable matte that reveals how the special effect was achieved.

Mattes

By simply cutting custom shapes, or mattes, in a video frame and overlapping footage with other scenes, computer artists can create many special effects without using chromakeys—though it takes some planning since matte elements typically need to be staged in the foreground of your compositions. Knowing when to use matte effects or chromakey shots (or both) is the greatest challenge of special-effects work. With some forethought, you can alleviate difficult matte cutting by shooting your source footage at the right perspective and expertly matching lighting and camera angle with other elements.

If you plan to show your final movie in black and white, you may still need to record scenes in color so that you can incorporate shots that require chromakey effects. In fact, it's generally a good idea to light and decorate all scenes for their chromatic properties—even when you intend to discard that color information later for sepia-tone or black-and-white presentation.

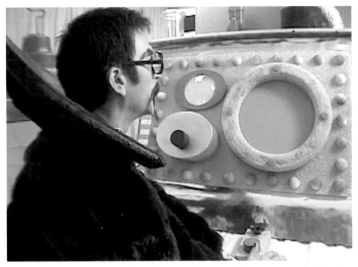

To matte or chromakey? That's the question! In this scene, an evil scientist peers into his magic porthole to view the actions of the hero. A simple circular matte could easily be punched out of the footage, revealing a video clip in the background.

Two actors share dialogue while a third man lies stiffly as a corpse between them, staged in the foreground and cropped to hide the movement of his body. Because the actor's breathing and blinking would be noticeable in close-up, a single frame was exported as a still image, a matte was cut to isolate the shape of the frozen face, and the matted photo was placed on top of the original footage.

However, because the actor's hand will pass in front of the porthole, a chromakey effect is used instead so that all of the elements of the scene appear more convincingly integrated. Although the footage will be converted to black and white in its final stage, chromakey effects make it necessary to design the scene with green-screen material and light it properly for the best color recording possible.

Controlling Motion

When a digital camera is stabilized, mounted on a tripod, or placed on a solid surface, the recorded images look very similar to static film frames (albeit there are more of them per second). It's only when the camera moves that video footage becomes startlingly different from celluloid. The tell-tale factor is motion blur, the unresolved images that wistfully trail behind objects as they speed through space. In film's 24-fps standard, motion blur provides an elegant transition between a progression of single frames, softening an otherwise jarring juxtaposition of images.

Video's heightened sense of reality, in contrast, is due to its higher 30-fps (or, more accurately, 60-fps) standard, which captures almost triple the amount of snapshots and allows for very little motion to become blurry—even at high speeds. Because more image information is articulated to the television tube, video signals tend to look sharper and glassier than film, missing the perceptible stutter found in motion pictures that have been telecined for broadcast. Also, film exhibits a tiny, shifting "float" which occurs because the film strip knocks against the gate of a projector, while video appears rock-steady to the seasoned cinephile.

To make video look like film, you need to drastically constrict camera movement. Oddly, vertical tilting doesn't betray the video image significantly; however, sudden horizontal movement, such as fast panning, is a nightmare for video moviemakers attempting to achieve film-like qualities.

Although there are workarounds, in general, a steady camera produces the most transparent, professional results. If you want your video to convey the feeling of a big-budget film, large-crew film, trade your handheld shots and Steadicams for a sturdy tripod, decent fluid head, weighted jib, and solid dolly tracking system.

Film Motion in Video Footage

Digital video footage borrows a filmic property through the use of shutter-speed controls, which change the rate at which fields are converted to frames, compacting the time between field sets and elongating the distance between actual frames. The slower the shutter speed, the more motion blur will occur in images. Thus, images captured at shutter speeds greater than 1/60th of a second show virtually no blur when projected, while those shot at 1/30th of a second will appear more like film.

You can also use a number of software plug-ins and applications (like Cinemotion and After Effects) to introduce motion blur into video footage to achieve a subtle amount of the movement typical of images projected on film. However, as in other digital post-production processes, your footage quality will deteriorate because of the interpolation of motion blur that occurs in such programs. For this reason, it's better to rely on your camera's built-in functionality to achieve these effects than to depend on the computer to fix wayward footage.

> **TIP**
>
> **SHUTTER-SPEED SETTINGS**
> CHECK YOUR CAMCORDER FOR ADJUSTMENTS THAT SLOW SHUTTER SPEED, A DIGITAL EFFECT THAT CAN REDUCE HIGH-SPEED CAMERA MOTION. IF YOU FEEL COMPELLED TO USE FAST PANNING DURING YOUR SHOOTS, YOU CAN EMPLOY THIS FEATURE TO IMPROVE YOUR COMPRESSED VIDEO.

Camera Movement for Web Video

Compression software doesn't like camera movement, especially things like fast tracking action. In addition, zooming is troublesome for Web video. Thus, if you're filming for the Internet, try to restrict your panning to short bursts—then settle the frame on its destination and hold it for a few seconds. This generally produces better streaming video. Instead of using your camcorder features to zoom in during videotaping, try to stage scenes so that you can take a static shot, pause recording, zoom in for a close-up, and then resume recording. Another solution is to have actors move within the scene to create several compositions within a single setup. This stabilizes many of the elements in the frame while providing the scene with new stages without additional camerawork.

Handling the Camcorder

Hand-held camerawork lends footage newfound mobility, interesting angles, and documentary-style vitality to your video—all of which make handheld shots a favorite for extreme sports, live news coverage, and music videos. Since holding a camera (even a lightweight model) can quickly bog down a camera operator, many of them use support devices and grip equipment. Although there are hundreds of choices on the market, almost any rig will ease the strain of carrying the camera on long takes. In the end, however, the best camera operators learn to stand still and reserve their jerky shooting techniques for the right moments.

Theres no need to shy away from hand-held shots; most of today's consumer-level digital camcorders have excellent built-in stabilization technology to reduce unwanted jitters. Nor should you worry too much about using products like Steadicam and gyro-based supports to smooth out motion: Your lightweight DV camcorder can easily reproduce the handheld takes produced by this type of expensive "professional" equipment.

Tripods, Jibs, and Dollies

Serious narrative filmmakers will find a sturdy tripod an essential part of their camera package. You should also research and invest in a fluid camera head for superior pan and tilt shots. A number of home-based businesses sell collapsible jib and dolly rigs that give the look of a professional crane in motion. These tools can help you establish excellent tracking shots and complex movement that flows freely throughout the set but is more consistent than a Steadicam or handheld shot. DV footage benefits extensively from these tools because their rigid construction prevents your camcorder's digital stabilization features from automatically interpolating frames to correct for sudden movement.

A special version of the popular gyro-based Steadicam system was designed for ultralightweight DV camcorders. Although learning how to use this counter-balance device takes some practice, it can help you glide through long takes that require handheld operation.

A jib is a weighted lever that sits on top of a tripod and allows for smooth tilt-and-swivel action. Combined with a dolly tracking system, this setup provides extraordinary freedom of movement in a variety of settings. Despite the tiny camera and fluid head mounted to the jib arm, supplemental weights help stabilize the moving system for a steady picture.

Silver Planet Studio

Carny Tales is one of dozens of DV shorts made by the gang at Silver Planet Studio, a digital effects production company I founded in 1995 to allow us to experiment with new tools and techniques. This 8-minute movie is the playful collision of two genres, blending the bizarre world of circus sideshow freaks with the gangland characters of a crime syndicate.

In this sequence from *Carny Tales,* a circus owner invites a young protégé into his office for a demonstration of his levitation skills. As he explains the art of levitation to his visitors, the child slowly lifts the grown man into the air. To "sell" the scene—that is, to make it believable to an audience—the man must appear to be suspended in space without means of support.

Although this effect might be achieved via an elaborate system of hanging wires and crane supports if it were shot on a Hollywood sound stage, here we used a simple-green screen set-up. Shot entirely on the miniDV format, the footage was manipulated using Primatte keying filters in After Effects.

SPECIAL EFFECTS WITH AN ORDINARY DV CAMERA

First, the circus owner was shot against a green-screen background. We then used a wide-angle lens to give the scene an otherworldly feel. The actor lay in a horizontal position to accurately portray the effects of gravity on his clothing and movement, balancing his body weight by placing the small of his back gingerly on a stool. The outline of the actor's body must remain within the color area of the backdrop, or subsequent matte processes will be extremely difficult.

Once the scene is shot, the footage is transferred to a computer and individual frames are examined to determine the most extreme areas of action. Then, a matte is cut to include all areas where the arms and legs may move during the entire video sequence. After the shape of the matte is found, the computer discards the surrounding areas.

Now that the matte has been cut, the actor can be repositioned to place his body in the most ideal portion of the frame. Chromakey software helps remove the green-screen background and create transparent edges around the contour of the body. A shadow is added with another software plug-in.

Another scene was shot in which actors pretend to see a floating man. It was important to use the same wide-angle lens that was employed for the green-screen takes. The actors in the foreground were instructed to keep their movements very rigid (for purposes of matte cutting), while the upstage actor was encouraged to use a full range of motion to create activity in the frame. This will help make the scene appear complex and lifelike.

Another matte is created using the source footage of the parlor room scene. Here, the foreground actors are left in their stationary positions, while the rest of the frame is made transparent. This process of matting without a chromakey is a simple solution used only when the background video is identical to the matted source. Cutting shapes for these actors takes some time, but it is not exacting work—the matte is loosely cut because it will not reveal telling details that spoil the effect.

The composite contains the parlor room video as the base layer. The circus owner (and shadow) are then placed in position, floating in the middle of the carpet between the other players. The last piece is the matted footage of the foreground actors, placed over the shadow and edges of the levitating man. At this point,

you can use software to microbalance the colors and exposures of each video clip to closely approximate a single lighting setup.

The old special effects masters in Hollywood used to talk about keeping things a little "rough," meaning that most audiences revel in the sight of fantastic visuals—even when they know it can't be real. Polished, computer-generated effects in feature films can lose their charm when they becomes too seamless. Thus, digital filmmakers should not feel that modest equipment and simple techniques will undermine their ability to present imaginative scenes through special effects.

chapter three
making a connection

Digital movie footage is really nothing more than a series of electronic files—extremely large files—and the best way to move those files is over a FireWire cable.

It's not without good reason that manufacturers of multimedia devices have adopted this high-speed serial data-bus technology. Offering transfer speeds of up to 400Mbps, FireWire does more than simply connect camcorders to computers; it enables aspiring directors to incorporate myriad bold, new peripherals, such as still cameras, audio mixers, and scanners, into the creative process.

FireWire does more than connect camcorders to computers.

FireWire also accelerates the performance of conventional equipment like hard disks and CD burners. As you venture further into digital moviemaking, you'll see that the benefits offered by FireWire are monumental: Easy cross-platform implementation, simplified cabling, and hot swapping are just a few.

When FireWire was introduced, it was limited in the cable distances it allowed and its ability to capture footage directly to disk while recording. But today most of those problems have been overcome, and a number of FireWire hubs, cabling systems, DV mixers, and signal converters allow you to use multiple devices and AV inputs for live events and direct Webcasting.

If you plan to purchase a DV camera, you should first check to make sure it includes an input for a FireWire cable—specifically, one that's labeled DV IN/OUT. Some early models were only able to carry data in one direction, thus significantly hindering your ability to export movies. If you wish to use your DV camcorder to convert analog sources into digital footage, pay close attention to the phrase *in/out* next to its composite video ports: Many models restrict analog-signal input, only allowing audio and video output.

iMac DV Computers Apple computers were the first to feature on-board FireWire ports. This iMac model was designed to give users easy access to the ports at the side of the system. However, most desktop machines keep the ports in the back, a frustrating place for busy filmmakers.

WHERE CAN I PLUG IN MY CAMERA?

If you haven't yet invested in a computer, make sure you get one that includes FireWire ports. The Mac remains a compelling platform for digital video production, and many Apple models pack extraordinary processing power, exceptional graphics acceleration, and plenty of hard disk space. These machines' moviemaking capabilities are further improved by built-in DVD drives, stereo sound, and preinstalled video editing software.

Since October 1999, Apple has shipped all its Macintosh computers with FireWire on board: Two built-in six-pin ports are integrated with the system software. If you own a recent-model Mac (from Power Macintosh G3 Blue & White computers to all iMac DV models, iBooks, G3 PowerBooks, and Power Mac G4 workstations and laptops), chances are FireWire ports are already included. Simply check the back of your system for the small FireWire icon above the port connector.

Today, most PC makers are following suit by including FireWire. In addition, Sony offers a number of affordable and complete Vaio systems, bundled with software and all of the connections required for speedy, seamless capture into editing applications.

BookEndz Docking Station This docking station eliminates the need to unplug all of the devices from your laptop every time you want to take off. Simply connect your Ethernet jack, USB devices, FireWire cable, modem, even an external video monitor to the docking station, and you have the equivalent of a permanent desktop system.

In/out ports Most digital camcorders feature FireWire four-pin ports, a durable inteface that can be plugged in any time—even while the camera is on and recording.

Plugging into Decks and Mixers

Many video professionals supplement their camera equipment with FireWire-enabled tape decks or video mixers, which can be connected permanently to the computer and act as a liaison between the camera and the video-editing application. Tape decks are used primarily for recording video from multiple sources, though many editors transfer DV tapes to decks simply to reduce wear on their cameras. These devices also save wear and tear of the operations of the camcorder, particularly the tape heads. In addition, many decks can convert analog signals to digital formats as well as perform simple insert edits and timecode-based recordings.

Mixers, on the other hand, allow editors to introduce real-time transitions and special effects to video streams *before* importing them into their computers. Most of them are used for live events or broadcasts, where decisions are made quickly and the real-time effects can be processed immediately. For the most part, these devices simply extend the digitizing process and are not required for simple DV moviemaking. If you intend to capture your footage into a computer, and add transitions or effects with the aid of a software application, there's no need to add a mixer to your home studio.

ADDING A CAPTURE CARD TO YOUR PC

If you purchased your computer prior to 1999, it's unlikely that it includes adequate ports for capturing DV footage. If that's the case, you can select from a growing number of add-on cards for Macs and PCs. FireWire capture cards not only allow you to transfer footage to the computer's hard drive, they also enable your editing software to control your camcorder functions and provide real-time input and output of DV audio and video.

DV-only cards Inexpensive DV-only capture cards provide a simple means of importing footage to PCs. This card plugs into the PCI slot of your computer and uses device drivers to guide video to and from software programs.

PCI Capture Boards

A video capture card is an add-on board that plugs into a PCI slot inside the computer and facilitates the import of digital media into your computer. While there are some cards sold as "cross-platform," it's a better bet to get one made exclusively for either your Macintosh or Windows systems, because the exchange of data at the motherboard level is the most likely place for information to become lost or damaged during transfer. Buying a card made and tested specifically for your system is safer than gambling on a one-size-fits-all solution.

Some inexpensive capture boards are meant to be used solely for DV capture. These cards are labeled "DV-only," which means they're geared toward capture from DV camcorders, and little else. Others, however, support analog *and* DV inputs, convert analog footage to DV, display real-time audio and video scrubbing, and support multichannel audio and real-time previews. DV-only cards, however, are more than adequate for most home-based moviemaking projects.

For professional studios and editors working under tight deadlines, more expensive solutions exist. Capture-card systems such as those from Media 100, Targa, and Matrox are commonly bundled with proprietary software and hardware that make quick work of computer-intensive tasks. Added memory and custom-made chips that accelerate frame rendering during transitions and/or special effects boost the performance of these cards. The trade-off, however, comes in price, which can be high since such cards generally support a range of functions: They supply a variety of input options; speed compression; support broadcast video formats; play back full-motion video at full-screen resolution; include character generators for titles; and cut waiting times for scaling, motion effects, color correction, and the editing of multiple streams. For beginners, these cards are overkill; however, they provide legacy PCs with the appropriate connections and processing power to meet the demands of digital video applications.

CardBus Adapters for Laptops

Laptop users may also need to buy adapters to turn any available CardBus slots into FireWire ports. Although dozens of suppliers offer mostly similar products, none feature the fancy connectors or powerful processing assistance available from PCI capture cards. Such cards do, however, offer solid DV-only throughput for direct import of video footage into notebook systems.

A word of caution: Many FireWire devices (particularly hard drives) draw their AC power from the system to which they're connected—not a problem with desktop systems. However, if you're running your laptop on battery power, it may not be

CardBus Adapter An IEEE-1394 CardBus Adapter turns your laptop or into a powerful FireWire machine: Simply insert the CardBus card into any Type II slot, and you can easily connect DV devices (camcorders, decks, still cameras, hard drives, and mixers) to your portable studio.

able to sustain the energy throughput necessary to keep these FireWire devices running, which means you'll need to do most of your editing within close proximity to an electrical outlet.

UPDATING YOUR FIREWIRE DRIVERS

Although both Macintosh and Windows operating systems now include a set of generic FireWire drivers to coordinate transfer to available ports, they often conflict with software supplied by third-party vendors and actually prevent you from using FireWire devices. Developers of FireWire peripherals are required to write and distribute their own device drivers, and when several drivers are being used simultaneously, or if a driver is not present, your peripherals may not respond properly. To avoid problems, make sure you periodically update your FireWire drivers and carefully follow the instructions for installing third-party drivers. You can do this easily by checking vendor Web sites and downloading the required software.

> There was an error while trying to initialise the video hardware.
>
> Please make sure the driver software for your video input device is installed properly, and that your device is not in use by another application.
>
> If you are using a FireWire video source please make sure a DV device is connected and switched on.
>
> [Quit]   [OK]

Device driver error The device drivers for FireWire peripherals may conflict with your computer's operating system pre-sets, or they may not work when a video application is addressing the FireWire port. If such is the case, check to see that you have the most current FireWire drivers installed and that no other programs are in use.

EXTENDING YOUR REACH

IEEE 1394-compliant FireWire cables deliver sufficient bandwidth to reliably transfer data in real time; thus, your video will not lose frames or corrupt your source footage. All FireWire cables should work with any FireWire device or peripheral. There are two kinds of cable plugs, each designed for a special purpose. Typically, cables with six-pin connectors move electricity from the FireWire bus to the connected device (however, some six-pin peripherals don't require any power). This is the reason that nearly all computers are manufactured with six-pin connectors, and that the ports reside in the back of the machine nearest to the power source. In contrast, four-pin heads (which were designed for tiny camcorders and other appliances) move data only: They can't supply a device with additional power. These smaller connectors are often found in the front of devices because they are easy to conceal.

FireWire Cable Length

Originally the maximum length of a FireWire cable was specified by an industry council as 10 meters (roughly 32 feet), but most cables lose their signal strength over such long stretches. That's why most cables used to connect one FireWire device to another generally aren't very long, and seldom exceed

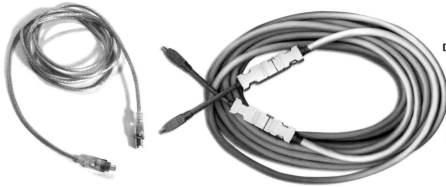

Distance DV cables You can extend your connections from the paltry 14-foot limitation of standard FireWire cables to 164-foot lengths. Distance DV cables include a filter and equalizer that reduces noise and attenuation to keep DV signals running longer on expansive sets, among office workgroups, and in multicamera live-switching production studios.

4.5 meters (14 feet). You should also remember that it takes power to sustain signal strength over long lengths; thus, a 10-meter FireWire cable must be connected to a hub or repeater on both ends if it is to draw sufficient electricity to retain a smooth data rate. Today, clever manufacturers have extended this limit by using fiber-optic cabling as a conduit. However, by understanding FireWire's limitations and following established guidelines for video transfer, you should be better able to troubleshoot problems on the set and keep your images pristine.

Using FireWire Hubs and Repeaters

While most FireWire computers, PCI cards, and CardBus adapters give you two ports to work with, you may find you need more as you add peripherals to your system. Thankfully, a slew of sleek and stylish FireWire hubs and repeaters extend this capacity, allowing you to link multiple devices on the same system. Theoretically, you can't attach more than 63 devices to a single FireWire chain, but hopefully your needs will never exceed this limit!

A hub is any device that adds more FireWire ports, allowing you to branch your devices to different ports so that you can unplug one set of devices without disrupting the flow of data to a set routed through another port. Of course, all devices must still be connected via FireWire cables. You *do not* need a hub to connect a camcorder to a single computer; however, if you wanted to make that camcorder accessible to five computers simultaneously, a hub would do the trick.

A repeater, in contrast, merely amplifies the DV signal, allowing it to travel farther; it does not split the signal into other ports. Typically used to link two cables, repeaters are only required if you need to exceed the maximum device-to-device FireWire cable length of 4.5 meters.

Because hubs and repeaters work well together, they're often sold as a single unit, called a *hub/repeater*. In this case, the hub simultaneously splits the signal into several ports *and* bolsters the signal strength (just as a repeater would).

Extending Your Ports The Belkin 6-Port FireWire Hub saves you the long reach behind your desk by placing connectivity at your fingertips. Just plug the hub into a single IEEE 1394 port on your Mac or PC, and suddenly you've got six FireWire ports. The innovative design allows the hub to stand upright or turn sideways to stack and chain multiple hubs.

Because hubs and repeaters don't require special drivers, you can plug and unplug them into any configuration. Although you don't need them to connect every FireWire device or cable, hubs and repeaters provide great flexibility and an important jolt of power.

Analog, Composite, and S-Video Jacks

If your camcorder or capture card readily accepts analog video signals from VCRs, television broadcasts, multimedia peripherals, and other camcorders, you'll probably need to convert the signals to a digital format before you bring them into your editing applications. But remember: When moving video between DV camera and computer, your camera has already done all the digitizing. Thus, many PCI cards designed for DV-only transfers merely capture, not digitize, footage. You may experience problems when importing analog footage through these devices.

Most DV camcorders and tape decks also have built-in copyright detection software that prevents the unauthorized reproduction of commercial material. This feature is a digital detective called Macrovision, which reads the electronic fingerprints of DVD discs and VHS tapes. Thus, if you inadvertently tried to import footage from a movie you rented at a local video store, a message would appear warning you of the infringement and the camera would stop recording.

Converting Analog Footage into Digital Signals

If you plan to use an analog camera or want to edit material from Composite, S-Video, Hi8, Betacam, or 8mm equipment on your computer, you have a number of options for making the analog footage digital—without using a digital camcorder. As previously mentioned, a wide variety of digitizing capture cards are available, ranging anywhere from $300 to $4,000. Although even inexpensive graphics adapters will do an acceptable job of getting old formats into today's applications, the most practical way to do so is via an analog-to-digital converter.

Converting Signals The Director's Cut converter by PowerR features two sets of analog outputs, which means you can import clips as you preview them on an NTSC television or monitor without swapping cables. It also supports the international PAL standard for input and playback. Best of all, it contains no Macrovision protection—that is, you can capture signals from DVDs, laserdiscs, commercial VHS, or digital cable TV.

Television Tuner Another FireWire digitizing converter, the Formac Studio includes a 125-channel stereo TV/FM tuner that allows you to capture radio and television broadcasts and keep them as CD- or DV-quality files.

Desktop Converter The consumer-friendly Hollywood DV-Bridge from Dazzle can also convert your old VHS tapes to high-quality DV video. You need to have FireWire ports on your computer, but the rest is easy. The upright form factor sits inconspicuously on your desktop and includes outputs for monitoring footage on a TV set. Best of all, it comes with simple editing software to help you get started.

Audio Mixer The MOTU 828 is a FireWire-enabled digital audio recording system with professional inputs for both Mac and Windows. It's an ideal mixer because its fanless hard disk recording mechanism is virtually silent and all signals are instantly converted and sent through FireWire to the computer or camera. It can power your external microphone and play back soundtracks without delay, so you don't need a separate mixer for portable recording, making the MOTU a perfect companion for laptop users.

Like the mechanisms inside digital video cameras, converters turn incoming analog audio and video into a DV-compressed digital stream—and export digital signals back to analog devices as well. Even better, they usually allow both signals to be input and output via FireWire, Composite, or S-Video jacks. The real magic of these devices, though, is that they convert to the DV format in real time—in essence making the analog footage appear as higher-resolution data to the receiving application. The converted footage can then be recorded to a Mini-DV tape, uploaded to a computer over a FireWire connection, or easily accessed by a digital editing deck.

Many converters are also able to mix several sources—which means you could plug in a digital voice track with analog background sounds, then output a combined signal of 16-bit, CD-quality audio to a DAT player or overdub it into a recording camera.

Linking Cameras

What gets lost in all of this discussion of capture and conversion is that DV cameras are simply wonderful devices to connect to one another. They serve as flawless recorders, ready to accept FireWire cables from other DV cameras and copy footage without any signal degradation. If you're keeping all of your media elements in the digital domain, you may never need to use a conversion device: Instead, you can simply employ your DV camcorder to capture and record from one tape or computer to another.

Recently, miniature cameras (most of them analog devices) have become the tool of choice for adventurous filmmakers wishing to shoot extreme sporting events or outdoor activities. By attaching ultra-lightweight helmet cameras or lipstick lenses, filmmakers can connect these electronic CCDs to the input jacks of nearby DV camcorders. They can then easily plug a FireWire cable into the digital camcorder and import the footage to their computers. This ambitious workaround has led to some exciting and innovative movies and has provided inspiration to a legion of thrillseekers hoping to document their activities.

POV Shooting This mini color spycam from HelmetCamera.com fits neatly into a housing mount that sticks with Velcro to almost any helmet, making it an ideal high-tech carry-on for parachutists, rock climbers, and skateboarders. Its video and audio cables connect to the mini-DV camcorder stowed in your fanny pack—which is also where the rechargeable battery sits, supplying five hours of recording time.

Rolf Gibbs

Taking the Shortest Route from Video Capture to the Web

Budding director Rolf Gibbs came up with a celestial idea. He decided to record a sky diver's point of view as he plummeted to the Earth. His concept was simple and elegant: Toss a 16mm camera out of an airplane, process the exposed film, and add narration from a poem about the mythical Greek hero, Icarus.

But free-falling is not as effortless as it seems. For one thing, the 150mph impact proved too much for most film equipment. So Gibbs went looking for "disposable" video cameras, eventually purchasing two Sony PC-1 digital handycams and interconnecting them by FireWire. The lens of the first PC-1 camera collected the footage and transferred the digital signals to another PC-1 at the back of a camera housing. Even as the front camera hit the ground, the rear camera continued to accept the last seconds without missing a frame.

The resulting short film, *G*, was much as Gibbs had originally conceived. It premiered at the 2000 Sundance Film Festival, demonstrating how a new generation of lightweight digital cameras can put sedentary audiences into the action.

The Bomb, a contraption designed to keep the camera lens face down, is held steady by expert sky-diver Dan O'Brien. Two 25-foot streamers are also attached to the housing to absorb vibrations from wind resistance once O'Brien lets go. This video footage was captured on a helmet camera worn by another parachutist.

After several failed attempts with 16mm and VHS cameras, Rolf Gibbs found a palm-size Sony PC-1 digital handycam for $250 at a pawn shop. He purchased another PC-1 online and linked the two cameras together with a FireWire cable. One camera placed in the nose of The Bomb absorbed the blow, while the other camera cushioned in the rear of the housing recorded the action using the high-speed video transfer technology.

At 30,000 feet, the movie begins. Gibbs scouted locations over Davis, California, in a Cessna airplane, choosing to shoot above foothills to give the landscape some distinction. He marked the position on a GPS system and instructed the sky-divers on how to initiate the camera functions before jumping. At this height, where the Earth's horizon can be seen curving in the distance, parachutists must slowly become acclimated to the altitude and breathe with oxygen tanks.

As the camera approaches 20,000 feet, the ground appears as a topographical map with murky browns and faded greens. The camera microphone records the shrill whispers of an intense wind. Although held by the hands of the diver, the housing spins slightly as it descends, lending the final footage a dreamy authenticity.

(continued on next page)

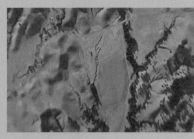

Near 10,000 feet, parachutist Dan O'Brien prepares to let go, and the Bomb will drift along on its own. By the time he reaches 2,000 feet, O'Brien must release and pull his rip cord; however, at this point, the camera housing will remain steady. Patchwork details in the landscape become clearer as the descent accelerates. Suddenly, the ground is moving toward the camera so fast that several minutes of falling seem to conclude in seconds.

Both 16mm and VHS equipment lost the ability to capture footage within the last 500 feet above ground level. Destroyed by impact at terminal velocity, those cameras either ceased to operate or exposed images beyond recognition. However, images captured with a FireWire  camera hold clear focus until the moment of impact.

Watching with binoculars from the ground, Gibbs tracked the landing within a quarter-mile of his position. Then, the crew drove trucks around the foothills to find pieces of the exploded housing. Here, Gibbs holds up the rear camera to show that it is operating properly and that the footage is unharmed. Immediately, the director was able to view his film with the crew. The director still uses the surviving camera.

chapter four
capturing and storing footage

Once you've connected all your DV devices, you're ready to "capture" or convert your video—that is, bring your clips into a computer so that you can edit the raw footage into finished movies. Video capture is the process of storing these clips (each a massive file) onto incredibly fast hard drives so that they're readily available for manipulation and playback inside software.

Before you begin capturing video, however, you need to understand two concepts: the way FireWire-based hardware devices such as cameras, decks, and PCI cards communicate with the computer to facilitate the transfer of files; and what the computer software does to measure and maintain the pristine quality of the original footage throughout your moviemaking efforts. Once you've grasped these basic ideas, you'll be ready to tackle more complex video productions like capturing live recordings straight to storage devices or recording to portable disks.

Because today's computers and software integrate technologies that speed digital video capture and encoding, getting clips from your camcorder is easy. However, once you've accumulated a large volume of media, you'll need to organize it. Clips can add up quickly, and some takes are hard to distinguish from others. This chapter discusses tools and techniques for logging, labeling, sorting, and indexing your footage so that you can quickly locate it years from now.

Once connected, you're ready to tackle complex video productions.

How DV Capture Works

When you transfer video clips from your DV camcorder over a FireWire cable, the computer doesn't alter the digital data. Instead, it simply moves the data from the tape to the hard drive—like copying a file from one location to another. Known as *capturing*, this transfer process differs significantly from the *digitizing* step required to convert video from an analog source. In the world of digital video, a *clip* is simply a data segment transferred for storage onto a hard disk.

Because digital video is compressed inside the camcorder, the DV data segments are seldom exposed to signal degradation. They are wrapped in a protective codec before transfer, and at no point will your editing software perform a function that would jeopardize the integrity of your original footage—not even when you apply titles or transition effects within editing applications. Usually, these applications will create a new file based on the original clip and merely outline the various changes to be made at a later time. Only when you're ready to export the final footage back to tape are the special effects and titles applied, at which time the application must unlock the digital signal to combine the original source footage with the rendered effects. Even then, the losses in quality that may occur in this process are minor enough to be deemed inconsequential.

Converting Footage over FireWire

When you import analog video from a converter box or special capture card, the footage is actually "digitized," meaning it will be changed from a modulated signal into a data file, forever locked into its current state of quality by a DV codec. For this reason, it's important that you use the best possible analog footage before beginning the digitizing process. Turning analog footage into digital data will not improve picture quality; it simply preserves the existing signal in a format that's impervious to further degradation.

Capturing analog footage through a converter works like this: First, the video is changed into data and compressed into a codec; then, it's transferred as a DV clip into the computer through a FireWire connection. This conversion takes place outside of the computer's own processor, using chips and circuits built into the devices or PCI cards that you have attached. Once digitized, all DV footage is protected by the computer and its applications to maintain optimum quality.

Importing Footage into Applications

To transfer DV clips to your computer, you'll need a capture utility—software that can detect FireWire devices and direct incoming footage to the proper storage space. Many such utilities include a Preview window for monitoring footage while it's being imported. They also often include on-screen controllers with buttons that emulate the play, record, stop, pause, forward, and reverse functions of your camcorder. There are several shareware and freeware versions of these utilities available online; however, it's likely that your editing software or PCI capture card comes preinstalled with such a utility. Most popular moviemaking programs such as Adobe Premiere and Apple Final Cut Pro include special modules that automate the import process and include settings for capturing by timecode or collecting footage in batches.

Apple's Final Cut Pro software contains a special window for logging and capturing your footage, giving you great control over the naming conventions and destinations of imported clips.

The moment you launch an editing application with a DV device connected to your computer, a status message will tell you whether the camera is turned on and a tape loaded.

During capture, the FireWire cable sends more than just footage to your computer; it also carries a host of information regarding the status of your camcorder and its footage, which enables your editing application to immediately sense when your camcorder has been connected or disconnected, if a videotape has been loaded or unloaded, and if the tape needs to be rewound. If the camcorder has not been turned on prior to launching an application, the program will likely generate a status message prompting you to adjust your camcorder operations before the import process can take place.

Updating FireWire Drivers

If an editing application doesn't immediately recognize your camcorder or DV deck, and you've made several attempts to resolve the problem (for example, checking the power source and tape and/ or removing the device from a chain), there may be a conflict between multiple FireWire drivers. Another possibility is that you don't have the most current FireWire drivers installed in your operating system. With myriad new device manufacturers rushing to introduce FireWire peripherals to a burgeoning market—and with each manufacturer required to supply its own drivers—conflicts of this nature are common. However, they're also fixable. Use your product documentation and the Internet to determine if your drivers are current. Most of the time, you can quickly download a driver from the Web and install it within minutes. To avoid problems, check manufacturer Web sites regularly to keep abreast of updates in driver technology.

PROBLEMS WHEN HOT-PLUGGING DEVICES

Usually, when a camcorder is *hot-plugged*—or attached via FireWire cable—to the computer, your editing application will automatically recognize the connection, making the video immediately ready for import. However, problems can arise; the following paragraphs cover some of the more common ones.

- *Some applications won't recognize camcorders connected to a daisy chain—i.e., a string of linked FireWire devices.* For example, Apple's popular iMovie software cannot import footage from DV camcorders attached via daisy chain. Likewise, many applications will not support the simultaneous use of multiple devices connected to your computer with FireWire because of driver conflicts. Typically, an operating system will assign a FireWire port to a single application at the exclusion of all other devices; when the application is shut down, the port is released for other uses.

- *Although most computers with six-pin FireWire connectors can supply adequate power to FireWire peripherals, this is often not the case with digital camcorders.* DV cameras require their own electrical sources and must be turned on with their own batteries or AC adapters before they are recognized by the computer and its applications. Unfortunately, the computer's internal power supply cannot supply sufficient DC voltage to operate a camcorder.

- *Never unplug a FireWire cable in the middle of a capture session.* Hot-pluggable devices are a tremendous convenience to computer users, but disconnecting them while importing DV footage can create a variety of technical problems—computer crashes, disk errors, damaged footage, missing data, and dropped frames, to name just a few. Make sure to stop your camcorder or finish your data transfer before removing a FireWire cable.

Device Control

In addition to recognizing hot-plugged devices, FireWire makes it possible for your software to operate your DV camcorder's primary controls from your computer screen—a feature known as *device control*. Rather than push the tiny buttons on your compact camera when searching for footage, you can manage your capture process from within the application, sending instructions to the digital camcorder with the aid of on-screen buttons that work as remote controls for record, play, stop, rewind, forward, and pause. This feature is ideal for scanning and playing back footage, providing the same level of frame-accurate control that professionals enjoy in professional editing suites.

Usually, capture sessions begin when the Play button has been selected and the desired footage is rapidly approaching. The operator then clicks an Import or Capture button (many applications use the space bar on your keyboard to start and stop import) and the DV stream is compiled onto the available hard disk space. Although this is an acceptable way of capturing footage, it often results in clips that are too long or too short, depending on the accuracy of the operator.

Marking Footage for Import

Many on-screen controllers allow you to set markers before importing a clip, pausing the camera functions so that you can select a single frame as the point at which the computer should begin transferring footage. Once you've marked an In point, you can resume playback, pausing the tape again to designate the frame at which capture should stop. In this way, you avoid importing excess data—a primary culprit in filling up precious storage space. Other applications go even further, memorizing the marker points from their timecode information as you scan the footage, then automatically capturing clips in a large batch while you leave the process unattended.

Most capture applications have on-screen buttons that provide remote control of your camera or its record, play, rewind, forward, and pause features. This feature is known as device control.

Whether you use a simple capture method or a sophisticated batch process with marker points, be cautious about the amount of footage you transfer to the computer's hard drive. Ideally, you'll want a *clean drive* to collect footage—by this, I mean a recently formatted hard drive or partition that doesn't include lots of little files. Generally, it's a bad idea to let the computer capture extremely long takes of video with the intention of chopping away unwanted footage; this can fragment the hard drive and adversely affect performance. Instead, take time to evaluate the video you're about to import and capture a series of shorter clips rather than lengthy, unbroken footage.

In addition, be aware of the limitations of your application and devices. If you use the capture session to explore creative options, you may end up with a rash of technical problems. Don't attempt to get slow-motion effects by "scrubbing" footage while capturing, or try to freeze a frame by pressing the Pause button while importing. Although in most cases, such actions will simply cancel the import, they could harm your system software and ruin your

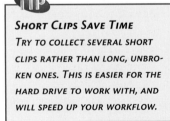

footage. (Besides, you can more easily accomplish these effects by using editing software.) It's also bad practice to unplug your DV device during a capture session because the sudden disruption will likely crash the application, damage the disk sector, or result in footage with missing data or dropped frames. Finally, don't try to capture video to projects saved on a remote server or to storage devices that reside on a network.

Viewing Your Clips

During capture, you may notice choppy playback and out-of-sync audio. Such problems are common because video playback on your monitor is refreshed only intermittently—that is, playback is put on hold while your computer's processing power is dedicated to making sure that no frames are dropped during capture. Once the capture session is over, the computer should resume normal playback. In many capture utilities, you can preview the video clips you have successfully transferred by switching the program into Preview mode or by simply double-clicking an icon of the imported clip.

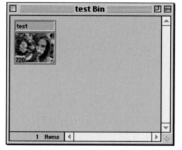

Many editing and capture applications offer bins to help you organize clips by scene or subject—handy for longer projects or when you're combining a number of other multimedia elements with your footage.

Saving and Backing Up

Before you begin to import, you should check your application settings for the destination of your clips. Each program saves video files differently, and many take extra measures to ensure safe storage. Many video programs "hide" the collected media files to prevent users from accidentally trashing important clips. Others automatically save files upon import or create

backup files to prevent the loss of footage in the event of a computer crash or power outage.

If you're not certain how your capture software is saving files, consult your documentation; this issue will become critical during the editing phase. Some programs leave a master file on the hard disk and generate separate clips every time you copy or alter a segment of video. Others will require you to manage and maintain the footage in all of its iterations—in which case you may need to make a backup of all clips before you begin adding effects. Backing up footage may take additional storage space, but it can also eliminate the need for recapturing scenes if the original files are destroyed or altered.

When Space Runs Out

Nothing fills up hard disks faster than video footage. You can avoid a last-minute space crunch by estimating the amount of storage capacity on local hard disks *before* you begin importing data. Digital video clips gobble up roughly 13 gigabytes of hard disk capacity for every hour of footage captured. Thus, if you wish to create a feature film on your personal computer (say, 90 minutes in running time), you better allow for at least 20GB of available storage space for the finished clips—and that doesn't include the extra space you'll need to review extra footage. It's not uncommon for editors to import four times as much footage as they actually need.

When disk space runs out, your software can't automatically seek out a new hard drive or remote volume and resume the capture process. In most cases, an error message will inform you that the disk is full and that the capture session has been terminated.

Maximum Length for Captured Clips

The maximum length of a movie is limited only by the available disk space on your computer; however, there is a technical limit on the file size of an individual video clip. Currently, Macintosh and Windows NT operating systems cannot create files larger than 2GB. However, there is no restriction on the number of 2GB files that can be combined to create the appearance of a single clip. Thus, many computer applications work around this limitation by presenting the user with an extended preview that is actually a series of smaller clips strung together by background procedures in the operating system. This workaround lets filmmakers view work with longer takes (a hallmark of the digital video revolution) and play them back seamlessly in their editing applications.

FireWire Storage Devices

If your project ambitions exceed the capture capacity of your internal hard disk, you may need to purchase additional storage space. Fortunately, hundreds of suppliers specialize in providing economical FireWire storage devices. As these manufacturers race to deliver faster read/write speeds and greater capacity for increasingly lower prices, competition is extending the use of FireWire hard drives well beyond the applications for digital video: These drives are even becoming part of new advances in automotive and medical diagnostic equipment.

Hard drives with ultrafast FireWire interfaces have also fueled the movement toward portability and network storage. The ability to write data quickly has made portable FireWire drives the device of choice among editors who favor mobile computers or who need to share their files. Portable drives provide an ideal way of offloading captured footage from a laptop or modest workstation, freeing up the internal hard drive for additional captures. Many filmmakers hand over their final digital movies to post-production facilities on these compact, portable hard drives, which also provide an easy way to share files, especially among team members who are not connected by high-speed networks.

Another unique advantage of FireWire storage devices is their interoperability with a variety of different computers. Macintosh, Windows, and Unix workstations all recognize FireWire hard disks the moment they're connected, making these drives a convenient way to swap files instantly. In

Portable FireWire hard drives, like this PocketDrive from LaCie, are ideal for filmmakers who need to offload clips from laptop computers, to retain a backup copy of important footage away from their desktop computer, or to hand over clips to post-production facilities.

contrast, almost all other storage devices have problems interfacing with multiple platforms. Part of the reason FireWire hard drives work seamlessly in all environments is that they're self-configuring devices—that is, all of the ID settings, termination, and switching are communicated over the cables to the host systems to which they're connecting. This helps them overcome any potential conflict with other peripherals on the computer chain.

Mondo Storage Devices

In addition to portable hard drives, the FireWire revolution has spawned a new line of massive storage devices able to share large amounts of footage among multiple workstations over a network. Although these huge hard drive enclosures (usually made up of several smaller drives) offer individuals a deep reserve of storage space (600GB or more), their real proliferation has occurred among small studios and workgroups.

With large storage volumes, a group of collaborators can set up a storage-area network (SAN), a small but mighty way to manage tons of footage and exchange clips among workstations (see Chapter 7). Much like a network server, the files that comprise a SAN can be accessed at FireWire or Ethernet speeds without copying individual clips onto a local hard drive. With

SANs, multiple users can make changes to clips while others are previewing the same footage simultaneously on another workstation. A perfect example would be the computer artist referencing the captured clips (not copying them to a computer, just creating proxies) and applying special effects while an editor in another office is referencing the same clips to create a narrative timeline. When the computer artist is finished, he or she can have the effects rendered directly to the clips on the hard drive. Once these effects are applied, they will appear—in their new form—in the editor's preview.

This type of mondo storage device often requires special formatting and disk management software, which also allows you to determine which users have read or write privileges to the volumes. These devices are quickly gaining popularity in interactive studios and broadcast design shops, where their network capabilities can significantly enhance productivity and workflow. Another blossoming area for these massive hard drives is live-event Webcasting, where adequate space

Inside the fancy enclosure of the 220GB MicroNet SANcube sits six speedy IDE drives with a unique traffic controller to send data quickly between the striped partitions and four FireWire ports—enabling multiple users to read and write data simultaneously.

and processing power are required to simultaneously capture a video signal, compress it for streaming, and transfer it to an Internet server for immediate delivery.

RAID Systems

If you've already invested in storage devices or have chosen to gradually work your way up to massive hard drives, you should consider the flexibility and affordability afforded by a RAID system. It's an awful sounding acronym for *Redundant Array of Independent Disks,* but as their name implies, RAID systems provide an inexpensive way to combine the performance of several low-cost drives without sacrificing the speed and reliability needed for disk access when capturing video footage. One factor that has made RAID drives popular is an overall improvement in the CPU speeds of today's desktop computers, taking the burden off of these devices to power and monitor the transport of data.

RAID drives are enclosures that hold multiple disks and write information sequentially across more than one disk. By dividing the load among several smaller disks, RAID drives allow a single volume to appear as larger than any one disk—when mounted on your computer desktop, the RAID volume appears to be a single, massive drive rather than several smaller drives. The number of drives that comprise a RAID system depend on the unit controller and how quickly it can respond to read/write sessions. Many of these units have redundancy operations that double-check passing information to ensure that no data is lost when recording video at high speeds.

Although you can build your own RAID systems using existing hard drives and inexpensive utilities available online, several manufacturers make preconfigured products in a variety of shapes and sizes. Most of the massive storage units used in corporate networks, Internet applications, and SAN workgroups are simply variations of RAID systems. Most of these systems feature SCSI interfaces to input and output data; however, several new models include FireWire ports. There are also a number of adapters that can turn existing SCSI interfaces into FireWire-enabled devices.

These sleek VideoRaid RT enclosures from Medea hold four 25GB drives, all controlled by RAID software. When connected by a SCSI interface to your computer, the drives appear as a single 100GB volume, ready for capture.

The VST RAID Array provides a clever way of turning several portable FireWire hard drives into one massive storage volume. By combining up to four 30GB drives, this tower can offer network access to 120GB of captured footage.

If your existing hard drive or RAID system is based on the Ultra SCSI interface, you can still connect it to your FireWire ports using a Ratoc FR1SX Converter.

Smart Storage Techniques

In video editing, the hard disk is the foundation of your workflow because it determines the responsiveness of playback and renderings. Indeed, you can dramatically improve the speed of your capture sessions—and the ease of your editing workflow—by following just a few simple rules for working with storage devices.

- **Don't partition your internal hard disk.** There's no need to divide a single drive into partitions for video capture. Keeping the operating system on a different partition can actually lower performance by forcing the drive mechanism to search for data between several partitions. Instead, just use a separate drive, dedicating an external FireWire hard drive for the collection of imported clips—a particularly effective solution for longer projects where you intend to use the maximum amount of available storage.

- **Leave some breathing room on the drive.** As the disk space on a storage device fills up, the drive mechanism begins to move slower. After accumulating hours of footage for your productions, you may find that your video playback (and perhaps your entire system's performance) is sluggish. Under extreme circumstances, your computer could crash repeatedly. It's best to allow a buffer of free space (no more than 10 percent) to protect hardware from undue wear and tear.

- **Format your drives periodically.** Disk drives take an awful beating while writing and rewriting data and searching for sectors and partitions. If you have a new drive, or if you recently emptied an older drive to prepare for video capture, reformat the drive using a drive utility. There are several new tools specifically designed for FireWire hard disks, which install special drivers to maximize throughput and increase playback performance. You can also use many of these utilities to help rescue files from damaged disks before formatting. Remember, formatting a drive erases the disk (wiping out all traces of previously written data), so be sure that your drive is clear of any important files before you begin.

- **Store project files separately.** If you've collected all of your captured footage onto an external drive, it's sound practice to store your application project files on a separate volume (such as the internal hard drive) as well as to keep any log files or edit decision lists along with them. By storing clips on a different drive, you avoid losing everything in the event of an irreversible disaster. If the external drive fails, you only lose the actual clips (which can be easily recaptured), not the entire project. It you've used proxies or reference files, your progress can be easily restored. Needless to say, it's always smart to back up your project files in a separate place (like a CD or Zip disk) on a frequent basis.

- **Be careful when deleting clips.** Several editing applications employ features that prevent users from mistakenly deleting clips. So there may be instances when you thought you had removed unwanted footage, only to find the Undo command will resurrect the clips from an unseen location. Because the deleted clips were easily restored, it means that they continued to reside on the hard drive while you went ahead and captured more clips. Once you have shut down application (or merely invoked the Save command) the application will empty its holding bin and finally clear the clip from the hard drive. But in doing this repeatedly, the disk can become fragmented and inefficient by packing the most data into the available space. If you are sure that unwanted clips will not need to be restored, make sure you have emptied the disk space by saving your projects, emptying any holding bins, or shutting down the program altogether.

LOGGING FOOTAGE

Novice filmmakers, especially those working on short video projects, seldom worry about logging their footage. They can capture with abandon and sort the files in the aftermath. But as experienced editors come to understand, lengthy projects demand a clear and consistent plan for organizing captured clips (and any other multimedia files that will be incorporated into a finished movie). Professional broadcasters use complex systems such as special database software to store, log, and label footage for use in multiple productions. Desktop editing tools, though not as extensive, still offer powerful features for keeping track of digital assets.

A brief overview of logging conventions such as timecode settings, batch processing, file naming, and image databases, will hopefully remove any intimidation that might have prevented you from automating your capture sessions. In the long run, proper logging methods can save you time and headaches.

Capturing by Timecode

In many modern editing programs, you can automate the import process by setting the application to capture the entire contents of a videotape, dividing the clips only by their timecode expression. Timecode is a unique numeric value embedded in the video signal that estimates the passage of time based on the amount of frames crossing the video playhead. When you record footage on a digital camcorder, the signal is permanently recorded with timecode data that always travels with the videotape.

Many DV capture utilities use this information to automatically determine when there's a break in the footage, and will import whole sequences by chopping up clips into the moments between unbroken timecode values—especially helpful when the clips you need to capture are generally free of lengthy stretches of unwanted footage. If this is the case, you can set the computer to capture an entire tape and leave the process unattended. Most applications can even sense when there's no more exposed tape (by the absence of timecode information) and stop the camera.

Timecode captures are great for editing event footage like weddings or picnics, where all scenes are related to the same location or theme, and the cameraman can occasionally turn off the camera or pause its operation. This way, the collected clips are all relevant to the event, and there are clear breaks in the timecode to clearly distinguish the clips.

Some filmmakers watch their footage with the timecode information displayed over the video to isolate the exact points at which the computer should start and stop a capture session.

Single performances like stage plays and speeches are not well suited for timecode captures because there are no breaks in the action and little reason to divide the footage into multiple clips. Likewise, sequences that involve repeated takes are not the best use of timecode capture.

Nevertheless, timecode can help editors in other ways. If you need to scour a tremendous amount of footage—let's say you want to isolate the best take in a shooting setup that involved 30 takes—you may want to view your video with the timecode displayed on the viewfinder to select the best segments. In fact, many filmmakers prefer connecting their digital camcorders to large TV sets (or copying their DV footage to VHS tape with the timecode display "burned into" the video) and scanning scenes from the comfort of their living rooms over using device control in front of a computer screen. After you've surveyed the tapes and recorded all of the timecode information for each clip, you can jot down the clock values for the beginning and ending of each scene and use this timecode information to capture clips in batches.

Batch Capturing

Batch capturing refers to several features that can save you time and frustration by automating repetitive tasks. Letting your computer import all footage by detecting a disparity in the timecode is only one way of batch processing; you can also set your application preferences to log clips into your project—assigning them with names and arranging them in sorted bins—before you even begin to capture them. If you've scanned your footage prior to capture, you can also key in the timecode values as a long list of In and Out points, and instruct the computer to collect them all in a batch.

In fact several programs, including Adobe Premiere and Apple Final Cut Pro, encourage you to import only lower-resolution proxies of your clips. This method involves scanning your footage, marking In and Out points, and labeling scenes and takes, as well as designating where files will reside. Once you've made your selections, the program will automate the capture of preview files (not full clips) and organize them per your instructions. By editing with proxy footage, you ensure that your playback and effects are extremely speedy and your hard disk space is better utilized until the project is finalized. When all of the editing decisions have been made, the program will recall the precise timecode markers, capturing the appropriate DV clips in full quality, and replace the proxies with real footage. This use of batch processing can be a real boon to productivity.

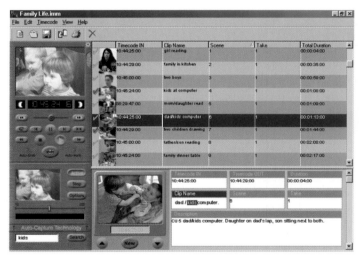

With DV Log Pro software from Imagine Products, you can automate your logging and capture sessions. DV Log Pro ferrets through your footage, divides scenes by timecode, and creates a set of thumbnails, noting the duration of each clip and leaving you room to write your own descriptions. Once you've checked off all of the clips you wish to import, you can begin a capture session or output a file that tells Final Cut Pro or Adobe Premiere how to execute the batch.

Naming Clips

In most programs (and in all operating systems), you can easily rename clips that you've imported into your computer. The way you name them, however, will affect your ability to track and manage your footage as it goes through the moviemaking cycle. Logging footage in batches automates the labeling of clips; however, it's wise to outline a naming strategy before you begin as well as to adhere to a few industry guidelines:

- **Devise a naming scheme that works for you.** Since file names should reflect the unique properties of the media within, avoid using generic terms or sequential numbers. For example, don't label your clips like this:

SCENE002_TAKE005_DIALOGUE.MOV
SCENE002_TAKE006_DIALOGUE.MOV

These names lack any real distinction and could leave you confused if the scenes were to suddenly become jumbled. The use of SCENE002 suggests that there could be as many as 999 scenes in your movie, an unlikely circumstance. What's more, "Dialogue" is a useless description since most footage contains some sort of speech or conversation. And unless you've got a mind like a catalog, remembering how TAKE005 differs from TAKE006 or dozens of other takes is nearly impossible from this naming structure. A better example might be:

BED_MAST2_CONFRONTS.MOV
BED_CLOS1_ROLLSOVER.MOV

In the above example the name is rooted in specifics. The scene is a bedroom, and even if the entire sequence is uprooted and placed at another part of the movie, the name doesn't refer to a specific order and thus loses none of its meaning. The word MAST can stand for a master shot in which the subsequent number indicates the number of characters present. Some editors even identify clips with clear-cut indicators like THEME or SFX to designate their purpose.

- **Keep vital information in the first eight characters.** Although most operating systems now accept significantly longer file names (anywhere from 10 to 26 characters), it's a good habit to keep key identifiers toward the front of a name: First of all, despite lengthier allowances in most file hierarchies, some editing programs restrict the number of characters in the small icons that display the name of a clip in bins or project timelines. Often this truncated name can't be longer than 10 characters. Second, if you should ever need to export an inventory of your media assets (for example, an edit decision list for post-production houses), it's likely you'll follow an industry format that sticks to a rigid naming convention (the dominant EDL format, CMX 3600, conforms all files to reel names of just eight characters).

- **Avoid including empty spaces in the file name.** Empty spaces and strange characters are often removed or replaced by the operating system or misread by other programs—especially when your files are moved to another computer. Parenthesis or brackets are often a waste of characters, when a simple underscore will serve to separate letters nicely. Slashes and hyphens also work well. To be safe, use standard character sets and try to keep your names from becoming unnecessarily obscure or cryptic.

- **Pick either upper-case or lower-case letters and stick with them.** The file architecture language used by nearly all computers does not differentiate between upper-case and lower-case characters. Thus, it's best to keep all names in one case or the other. This will prevent you from inconsistencies when using automated features that supply file names sequentially or when typing a series of names in by hand. Inevitably, you'll someday have to search for clips in a long list of file names, and you'll thank your lucky stars that you chose a single case and stuck to it.

- **Use commonly accepted three-digit file extensions.** The widely used format standard for extensions is a three-letter code separated from the file name by a period. Follow these extensions as you would on other media files, and conform to their use, as in the following file names:

TITLE_CRED6_PRODDESIGN.PSD
TITLE_CRED6_PRODDESIGN1.EPS
TITLE_CRED6_PRODDESIGN2.EPS

The first name could refer to a title-card graphic in the credit sequence identifying the production designer. As an Adobe PhotoShop document, the file name carries a .psd extension that could signal to the editor that the file contains layers of text that can be animated separately in programs like After Effects, Premiere, or Final Cut Pro. However, if the editing software did not accept layered files or was unable to recognize the .psd extension for import, the editor might have the option of using two Adobe Illustrator files and animating them individually. In this case, the file extensions in the name save the editor time in troubleshooting incompatibilities.

Needless to say, if you're working with other members of a team, you'll need to communicate and monitor the use of naming conventions to reap the long-term rewards of this organizational tool. Furthermore, if you're working across a network or shared file server, these naming tips can also apply to the folders and bins that harbor your media files. Be careful to give unique names to each folder and bin within a project, or you may find that after archiving several movie in a database system, your search results list the same name for similar elements in very different projects.

MEDIA MANAGEMENT TOOLS

The proliferation of digital creation tools coupled with the falling costs of mass storage has produced a glut of haphazard media stockpiles. At the conclusion of a project, artists usually throw all of their digital assets (project files, layouts, logos and graphics, video, audio, and text elements) onto a removable cartridge or perhaps burn their contents to a compact disc—and subsequently dismiss the matter. Inevitably,

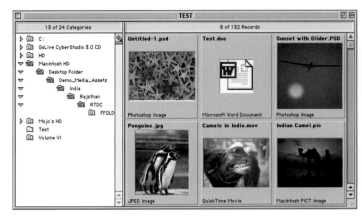

Media asset management software, like Canto Cumulus, offers an easy way to catalog the multimedia elements used in your movie projects—graphics, audio, video, and text files—and creates a searchable index using keywords, notes, voice annotations, and picture icons.

though, filmmakers will return to this mounting pile of discs and videotapes to find a clip or to reuse a sound effect. You can make use of much of the preparation that went into logging your footage at the capture stage to create a permanent record of all files in an searchable catalog or index.

This method of tracking clips—known as *media asset management*—is critical for large broadcasting organizations such as news studios that must instantly recall an interview or photo from a vast collection of material. Thankfully, there are several simple yet powerful tools for both the Mac and Windows platforms that make it easy to track assets residing on your computer or tucked away deep in a pile of discs. Most include a powerful search engine that locates a clip or file by keyword or by naming convention, drawing vital data about duration and formatting from the digital file itself. Many such tools enhance their searches with picture previews and short audio samples, and allow you to add voice annotations to file descriptions before generating slide shows or HTML pages so that you can browse or publish an entire catalog of assets quickly and conveniently.

To catalog assets, you don't need to archive them all in the same location. In fact, most catalog software simply creates a thumbnail or icon of an element and logs the name of the

CD or tape where it resides. Some filmmakers shun complex software and instead use a shareware indexing tool or simple database program for tracking assets. However, large companies with deep reserves of media hosted in remote locations will likely need a more robust system for updating their catalogs. Either way, media management tools provide an effective way of organizing, locating, and repurposing your footage.

Capturing Straight to Disk

Because the components inside digital camcorders instantaneously turn moving pictures into data, there's really no delay in the time it takes to record this pixel information to any device. This means that a DV camcorder can send live footage to a hard disk just as easily as it writes data to a tape. Therefore, some capture sessions, such as live events or studio shoots that involve multiple camera angles, can circumvent a videotape and record images directly to a hard drive. Because a direct-capture process requires high-speed throughput of data, filmmakers seldom employ this method without hard drives equipped with ultrafast SCSI and FireWire-based connectors.

Direct capture is practical for filming live events that must be quickly compressed and streamed to the Web, or for mixing two or more video signals from different cameras into a single broadcast. Under these circumstances, the time it takes to scan or log footage causes an unwelcome delay. However, the direct-capture method is impractical if you're not working under such pressing constraints, since this method fills up storage space very rapidly and places great demands on the computer's CPU.

Obviously, direct capture is a precarious practice: If the computer crashes during live recording, the entire session will likely be lost. For this reason, many filmmakers choose to keep a videotape rolling and pass the data to a hard drive. This way, they have a backup version on tape while still meeting the immediate needs of live broadcast.

Using Measuring Equipment

If you intend to capture live events for broadcasting, you may need to measure your video signal with an *oscilloscope* to ensure that it meets television standards. This hardware device displays the signal strength of analog video so that you can evaluate levels of brightness and color that can be technically reproduced on most TV sets. If you're using digital cameras in combination with analog cameras, both signals must conform to the "legal" limits of an analog broadcast before going on the air.

Oscilloscopes used in video monitoring generally come in two variations: waveform monitors and vectorscopes. A waveform monitor gives a visual display of the luminance levels in video footage, while a vectorscope focuses on the chrominance, or the range of color values, present in the signal. When combined with a signal modulator or processing amplifier (usually called a *proc-amp)*, the waveform and vectorscope can help you modify the video signal so that it falls in line with broadcast requirements.

Waveform monitors are primarily used to measure the voltage in a video signal to ensure that exposure levels don't exceed 100 percent level at the brightness point in your images or drop below 7.5 percent at the darkest point. Signal levels that appear too high on a waveform monitor will look hot-white in areas that have been clipped off at the top of their waveform spectrum. Low levels also appear clipped on the monitor but show up in the video as completely black.

Reading these levels, however, is quite different from correcting them. To do the latter, you need a processing amplifier that can actually adjust the signal strength of the video as it's transferred from one device to another. When using a proc-amp, it's best to keep white areas in the 90 to 100 percent range displayed on the waveform monitor so that the video will retain some detail. Darker areas—that is, those that fall under 30 percent of the signal strength—should not fall beneath the 7.5 percent mark. When measuring video signals, professionals are most concerned with skin tones, which appear around the 70 percent range in the waveform monitor and help match actors' facial colors from shot to shot. Keeping skin tones consistent is difficult when matching several video sources without equipment that monitors brightness.

Waveform monitors and vectorscopes have traditionally been used in the analog TV world but have seldom been employed in the fledging field of digital video production. Several factors have contributed to the slow adoption of measuring equipment in DV projects: For one, this measuring equipment is bulky and complex, making it counterintuitive for guerilla filmmakers using lightweight cameras. In addition, if a project is destined for CD-ROM, Internet video, or film transfer, there's little need to make the images conform to broadcast standards. And many cameras include features like zebra patterns and IRE indicators to help filmmakers gauge when their exposures are reaching the extreme range of luminance.

If you're using a capture card or digital converter to bring analog signals into a computer, waveform monitor and vectorscope devices can help you match the signals from source to source. Some filmmakers are finding these oscilloscopes helpful when shooting video that will be transferred to film, and are bringing the monitoring equipment on locations. But because this equipment is too expensive for the home user, many editing applications now include software modules that emulate the functions of oscilloscopes.

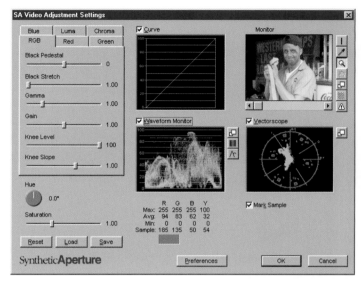

The waveform and vectorscope monitors built into Final Cut Pro and Premiere are simply software emulations of the traditional measuring devices used in broadcasting studios. However, they can aid only the desktop editor who is digitizing footage from an analog source, and they offer no control over signal modulation.

Additional plug-ins, like Video Finesse from Synthetic Aperture, can help you adjust the chrominance levels and luminance ranges of your video footage during capture.

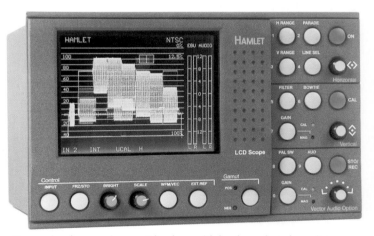

Proper signal processing must be done with hardware-based monitors working in concert with a processing amplifier (or proc-amp) to ensure the video remains within the "legal" limits for television broadcast. This FireWire-based scope from Hamlet works with an LCD display instead of a CRT, which can often introduce troublesome focus, astigmatism, or parallax problems.

Do I Need to Use a Waveform Monitor or Vectorscope?

Oscilloscopes are well-known in television broadcast circles, where they help technicians adjust the signal strength and luminance values of multiple sources of analog video to match one another and keep their programming within acceptable industry ranges for color and brightness.

However, this equipment is seldom used in digital video productions because many of the camcorders on the market do an excellent job of recording and maintaining these ranges. And, frankly, many newcomers to the DV revolution have only a faint understanding of the broadcast guidelines, so they are reluctant to endure the cost and complexity of measuring devices. In many cases, they may not have the need for them. Here are few ways to tell if your project can succeed without a waveform monitor or vectorscope:

- *Your project uses digital video exclusively.* If you're not combining DV footage with an analog source, you won't need to overcome glaring differences in luminance and color, which means that measuring equipment may not be necessary.

- *All of your DV footage was shot and captured with the same camera.* If you shot all of your footage on the same camera and intend to edit the entire project on the same system, the issue of signal quality may never come up. Most brightness and chrominance problems occur when footage is moved between different devices and editing systems. If you intend to export

the finished movie to the same DV camcorder, the file is simply copied as data without affecting the recording levels.

- *Your project is not intended for broadcast TV.* If your movie will only be seen on a computer monitor, CD-ROM, or an Internet streaming media player, issues surrounding signal strength are moot. Computer CRTs display pixel information instead of waveform signals and therefore don't adhere to broadcasting's strict demands.

- *You're monitoring levels with zebra patterns in your camera's viewfinder.* If you are at all conscientious about the extreme ranges of exposure and brightness during recording, it's likely your footage will fall safely within TV's preferred range. Use the zebra patterns or IRE indicators and follow the documentation for your camcorder to monitor these levels in the viewfinder. Finally, projects that involve nothing but digital video clips have little problem matching values from shot to shot. However, if you're using After Effects or 3D applications to generate original animations and then compositing these graphics with DV clips, your footage may have a different luminance range than your digital video. Often the work can appear washed out and foggy after it has been rendered. In this case, you may need to adjust the brightness and contrast settings to align the levels with the luminance range of your video clips. Also, use test patterns to help examine these levels on a reference monitor.

For instance, Premiere and Final Cut Pro both contain waveform and vectorscope windows that let you modify the color and brightness levels of incoming video as you digitize. Unfortunately, changing the signal modulation of a converted analog stream is a fairly sophisticated procedure, so amateurs should do a little research and practice on sample clips before applying changes to a large amount of clips.

Note that software-based waveform, vectorscope, and proc-amp processes only need to be applied to incoming analog video signals. Once analog video is converted to digital data, you can't modify the signal strength of DV files, only their chrominance and luminance levels. Generally, digital camcorders do an excellent job of recording and maintaining proper levels and signal strength, so the waveform modules inside today's nonlinear editing programs are rarely used.

Capturing Live Video from a Camera

Some cameras simply cannot record images to a standard tape format—either the camera is of such high resolution that the tape's limitation will force the frames to drop color information, or the custom proportion of the frames cannot conform to the convention aspect ratios of videotape. When shooting with this kind of specialized equipment, the only option is to record the digital footage directly to a hard disk.

Some digital cameras, like the Ikegami HDL-37, have no internal tape mechanism. This compact FireWire-enabled camera delivers outstanding three-chip quality for high-definition television, but its 2-megapixel images must be captured straight to disk.

Most digital cameras, however, will pass data through FireWire ports, even as they record footage to videotape. But if you intend to capture live video from a consumer-level DV camcorder, you may have to trick the camera into the act: With many DV cams, you'll have to switch the settings to Camera mode and set the Lock/Standby switch to Standby.

The revolutionary Be Here iVideo lens can record 360-degree moving images that allow a viewer to spin the video and interact with the scene in any direction. The special requirements of this digital camera and its custom aspect ratio mean that high-quality footage must be captured straight to disk and archived on hard disks.

At this point, you can often remove any tape cassettes from the camera, which might cause the camera to time out or go into Sleep mode. If your camera requires that a tape be in the camera but does not seem to be sending video data through the FireWire cable to a computer, check to see that the tape's write protection tab is unlocked. Also, make sure that the camera's Demo mode is disabled, because some cameras will automatically switch to a Demo mode when left on standby without a tape inserted.

Recording Straight to DVD

Who says you have to capture to a hard disk? Today, there are a variety of DVD-RW mechanisms that will accept digital video or analog conversions over a FireWire cable and burn the footage directly to a write-once DVD-R disc or rewritable DVD-RW media. You can hook your digital camcorders directly to these devices and record footage straight to DVD discs—even without a tape in the camera. Unfortunately, the pristine DV signals are recompressed to the MPEG-2 format, but the whole process happens on the fly and produces extremely high-quality video for immediate DVD playback. Just imagine burning footage with the timecode information displayed onto a DVD disc, and sitting back on the couch logging scenes with freeze-frame accuracy.

Pioneer's consumer-friendly DVD recorder, the DVR-7000, looks like any other VCR you might find in your home. But when it's time to record, the DVR-7000 uses FireWire and analog inputs to burn video signals onto write-once DVD-R discs or rewritable DVD-RW media—even taking footage straight from a DV handycam.

Damaged Californians

When a group of Los Angeles independent filmmakers called Damaged Californians joined forces with a local university and television station, they added a special incentive for runners participating in the city's annual marathon. In addition to broadcasting footage of the race, they announced plans to compress and publish each athlete's victorious final moments on the Web the very next morning. For the first time, a major marathon would let tens of thousands of nonprofessional runners witness their personal accomplishments.

With the help of UCLA, the Damaged Californians pooled together the processing power of today's cutting edge computers and applications to deliver on their promise. On Sunday, March 4, 2001, the digital cameras began rolling as the first runner crossed the finish line and continued to role for 5½ hours until the majority of runners had finished the grueling race. And sure enough, within 24 hours, every person's winning moment was available on the station's Web site. The campaign, called "Your Winning Finish," was an instant smash.

FILMMAKER PROFILE

TAKING THE SHORTEST ROUTE FROM VIDEO CAPTURE TO THE WEB

To record all 27,000 LA Marathon runners as they crossed the finish line took more than six hours. Cameraman James Keitel sat on a press dias at the end of the race. Here, he monitored a rolling Sony TRV900, looking for breaks in the action so he could quickly change tapes as they approached the 60-minute mark.

Then, Dmitry Kmelnitsky and Scott Hessels brought the tapes to a media lab on the UCLA campus and began capturing footage. They dismissed more powerful applications like Final Cut Pro and instead chose Apple's iMovie software for its simplicity. Instead of batch capturing the video by timecode, the D-Cals watched the race clock in the footage to break the clips into five-minute segments, simply hitting the Space Bar to stop and resume the capture process.

After moving the individual clips over a high-speed network to another computer, they set up batch process using Media100's Cleaner 5 software, which automates several time-consuming steps. Complicating matters was the fact that an important corporate sponsor wanted its logo embedded in every frame of the video clips before they were posted. But Cleaner was able to compress a dozen clips at once in two different codecs, embedding a logo on each frame of the video streams, naming and posting the final files to a designated FTP server for immediate Web access. This process was duplicated on several computers simultaneously.

(continued on next page)

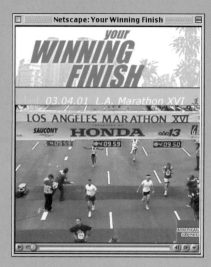

Because Kmelnitsky had prepared HTML documents in advance, including the reference names of the incoming files, the clips were instantly accessible once they were transferred to the streaming server. Each clip was compressed in both fast-streaming Real video files and higher-quality downloadable QuickTime movies, and placed inside a window matching the overall site design.

The final Web site was completed just 24 hours from the start of the race, giving more than 27,000 runners a unique view of their amazing accomplishment. Every person's winning moment was available on the station's Web site as a streaming file or downloadable clip that they could email to friends and family. The site

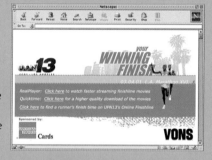

collected more than 1½ million hits in one week, and the station was deluged with messages from thrilled runners.

chapter five

previewing and
editing projects

There's nothing as rich in possibilities as having your clips finally gathered together inside the computer, ready to be assembled into a finished movie. From here, you can experiment endlessly with transition effects and special filters to shape your raw footage into a pictorial language—all the while retaining the picture quality of the original. One of the great advantages of digital video is that it allows you to edit your clips together in countless combinations, cutting and recutting, without risking damage to the master footage files.

Previewing is the only way to gauge how effects will appear.

If you intend to keep your project entirely within the digital domain (creating Web video or CD-ROM discs), you may never need to speculate how your movie will look to audiences—what you see on a computer monitor will be remarkably close to what others see when they view it. But if you eventually want to see your final movie on TV (via broadcast or VHS tape) as most filmmakers do, previewing your projects is the only way to gauge how your effects will appear on the TV tube. This is because TV sets operate very differently than computer monitors. And video displays radically differently in software applications compared to how it looks when it's transferred to a DVD disc or played back on a VCR.

Thankfully, FireWire technology can help you at this stage as well, thanks to the two-way transmission of video and information. While you work in an editing program, FireWire ports or camcorder connections enable you to preview sequences on a television set. Furthermore, a host of other FireWire products are now available to help during the editing phase. FireWire speakers, scan converters, and playback cards all enhance your ability to accurately preview work before deciding on your final cut.

This chapter details the steps you must take to ensure success with video playback. We'll take a quick look at popular editing applications, as well as optional software that can help you preview clips using your computer and external devices. Unfortunately, there's not enough space here to examine every editing program in detail, but understanding how these applications present your footage on monitors will prove valuable as you complete your movies.

OPTIONS FOR VIDEO PLAYBACK

Imagine the horror of working for days (or weeks) on a project and suddenly seeing glaring errors in the final film for the first time on a TV set. Thankfully, editors have the ability to preview images before they reach the final stages of production. Previews come in several forms. Some editors simply use software players available in video editing applications to preview clips on the computer display. Others use special video cards to stream previews to TV monitors adjacent to their desktop system. However, FireWire technology recently has replaced the need for these cards by streaming the footage directly to equipment so that you can see what clips will look like on television—long before you make your final edits.

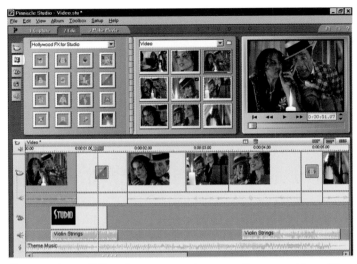

If you purchase a PCI card you may receive a complimentary video editing program like Pinnacle System's Studio 7. While these intuitive programs are designed for novices, don't let their simple interfaces fool you: These powerful tools meet all the requirements of movie production.

Preview Frames

In many editing applications, the easiest way to preview your captured clips is by switching the program into Preview mode or simply by clicking an icon of the imported clip. But when you watch these clips on screen, images often appear pixilated, dark, or muted in tone when represented at full size. This is because most computers are not nearly powerful enough to display full-screen motion at real-time speed, so each clip is given its own set of low-resolution preview images. To get around this problem, PC manufacturers and software developers have developed *preview frames*.

As a computer captures a DV clip, it creates a set of preview frames to simulate the motion of the source footage without disrupting its protective codec. In creating these previews, the computer quickly distills the millions of colors in the original footage into a limited palette that will display best on your

Apple's iMovie software presents users with large icons that represent each clip. When you select them, their associated clips appear in the Preview window, where they can be "scrubbed" (played forward or in reverse) by dragging the playback marker back and forth with the mouse.

screen. Your editing application or capture utility determines which computer format will be used for these preview frames (QuickTime and AVI formats are among the most common). However, regardless of format, such previews never affect the ultimate quality of the original video codec. Preview frames make up the clips you see in your editing applications. In fact, you'll never actually see a pure DV stream on a computer monitor—only a television set can accurately display the real video signal.

In addition to creating preview clips, editing applications must send the original DV footage to an output device on your PC (this can be through a FireWire port or a PCI card), so that you can see the video displayed on other devices attached to your system. For instance, if your digital camcorder is still connected to the computer via a FireWire cable, it's likely that any files you previewed on your monitor will also appear in the camera's viewfinder. Commonly referred to as *pass-through playback,* this feature can be turned on or off by setting the preferences of your editing application.

WHY DOES MY FOOTAGE APPEAR BLOCKY?

Once a computer has imported DV footage, it keeps the original source files on the hard disk and creates a series of preview frames to display in the editing application. These preview frames are created by removing much of the video and color information that NTSC televisions require, and simply displaying the frames as they will best appear on your computer monitor.

Although these images will appear blocky, fuzzy, or more muted than those seen through the viewfinder of a camcorder, not to worry: These screen images are simply low-resolution stand-ins for the real footage. Once formatted, these preview frames will appear at full screen and full motion, and display much faster than the higher-resolution images of an uncompressed video stream.

Previews make the long and arduous task of editing infinitely more bearable by speeding the response time of video playback. Without these low-res substitutes, even the fastest computers would be unable to display motion pictures in real time. Meanwhile your full-quality original footage remains locked inside the clip by the DV codec until you're ready to export your final movie in all its glory.

Editing Application Overview

Editing applications generally follow one of two metaphors: the user-friendly video workshop or the all-inclusive movie factory. Programs in the first category, like iMovie, appeal to newcomers because they're limited in functionality and avoid complexity at every turn. These straightforward tools usually feature drag-and-drop icons and present large buttons as a way to select a desired effect. They hide their power behind a facade of simplicity. Designed to remove any intimidation from the filmmaking process, most such interfaces succeed in making editing a fun and stress-free experience.

Other applications, like Adobe Premiere and Apple Final Cut Pro, hail from a long line of professional nonlinear editing systems and a legacy of broadcast techniques. Their development has been years in coming, and along the way their feature sets have been both streamlined and enhanced to give editors greater control and flexibility—at the cost of complexity. These environments are not immediately intuitive (in fact, novices may find them a bit daunting); however, they do allow users to fine-tune almost every aspect of digital production. You can alter the colors of clips, the behavior of text, and almost every variable of your special effects and transitions. However, in the process the interface often becomes convoluted with cascading windows, tiny buttons and sliders, and submenus that can easily overwhelm the casual user. Making matters even more confusing, several of these popular programs have recently added compositing modules and special effects controls—both previously the exclusive domain of separate applications.

This movement toward all-in-one editors has created some two-headed monsters: programs that can do it all but demand tremendous processing power and substantial computer memory. Many of these applications also depend on the use of third-party plug-ins to extend their capabilities, which has made managing software and hardware configurations a complicated prospect.

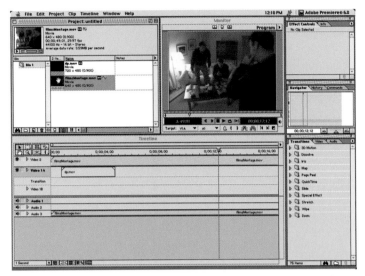

Video editing stalwart Adobe Premiere can boast compatibility with the widest range of software plug-ins, third-party filters, and file formats.

Apple found immediate success with Final Cut Pro by integrating it with core technologies on the Macintosh platform, namely QuickTime and FireWire.

Media100 (an Avid subsidiary) has transformed EditDV into a full-blown video environment by adding a number of Web-compression and batch-capture functions to gobble up market share among corporations using streaming video to reach customers.

Final Cut Pro, for example, is a professional package with an extensive set of special effect filters and titling controls, but it doesn't run efficiently on any Macintosh model with less than 450 Mhz speed and at least 256 Mb of RAM. Nevertheless, the software quickly made inroads in the broadcasting world because it followed many of the conventions of established editing programs and incorporated titling and compositing functions previously found only in separate, stand-alone applications.

Avid's Xpress is another example of a high-end editing application. This software was once the industry darling, dominating most high-end post-production facilities. Until recently, the software was only available bundled with a souped-up system, completed by some proprietary enhancements. However, today's computers can finally meet the demands of this award-winning digital video editing interface, and the Xpress DV software is now sold independently of its hardware.

Both the simple or the complex editing program can give the everyday computer user enough functionality to create short films or full features. Pick one, and you'll likely never need another: That's because those drawn to simplified interfaces tend to stay away from programs with more extensive capabilities. And those who choose more sophisticated applications invest so much time in training they're unlikely to jump to a competing product.

PC users can find an alternative to Final Cut Pro in Sonic Foundry's Vegas Video, an all-in-one program that tackles sophisticated titles, motion tracking, and special effects without leaving the editing environment.

Touted for use on laptops (pictured here on the FireWire-enabled IBM IntelliStation), Avid's Xpress software includes an impressive set of NLE capabilities, effects, audio, titling, graphics, compositing, and features for easy Web streaming and DVD delivery.

Of course, you don't need an editing application simply to play video clips on a computer. You can use a software player instead. Most modern operating systems include a media player that reads and displays a variety of file formats. Apple provides the QuickTime Player utility as a handy tool for translating and viewing hundreds of audio and video formats, while Microsoft distributes a similar program called Windows Media Player. These players are essential components of most video editing systems because they provide the underlying architecture for multimedia playback during editing.

Although both QuickTime and Windows Media players allow you to view video files compressed for Internet streaming, other players exist that are designed solely for viewing Web movies. The RealVideo player is a browser plug-in developed by RealNetworks to provide a means of efficiently streaming video over low-bandwidth Internet connections.

However, you cannot download or save streaming files viewed through the RealVideo player because they reside on a secured server that prevents unwanted copies from being distributed or collected.

DEVICE OPTIONS

If you're making a movie that may find its way to a TV station or cable network, you need to be particularly aware of some guidelines that all broadcasters must follow when distributing video programming. Although these federally mandated restrictions vary from country to country, they all exist for the same reason: to ensure that every signal broadcast to a television set falls within the range required for standard picture quality. These ranges were established to overcome the large variances found in the thousands of analog television sets, each made by a different manufacturer.

Although it's nearly impossible to tell what your movie will look like on a given TV, by staying within these guidelines, you can be sure your video images will fall within acceptable

With the RealVideo player, you can view movies streamed over the Internet. But unlike the QuickTime and Windows Media players, the RealVideo player cannot translate file formats or save video that has been streamed from a secured server.

norms. Do you *have* to follow federal TV guidelines? Yes, because many broadcast facilities can determine whether your video signal is "legal." If it's not, many stations or network engineers will reject it. If you're shooting a commercial for a national advertisers, or want to show a project over a public broadcasting network, you should take steps to ensure your video signals will be received without a problem.

Unfortunately, there's nothing you can do to a computer screen to accurately view the "legal" limits of video footage for broadcast purposes. For this reason, all filmmakers should attempt to preview their footage on a TV monitor during the editing stage. To do that, you need a reference monitor.

Reference Monitors

There are two kinds of analog video monitors. One is designed to show programs to an entire family in the living room; that's called a TV set. The other is designed to represent an accurate video image to help broadcast engineers analyze picture quality; it's called a reference monitor. This kind of monitor, which is also sometimes called a production monitor or broadcast

Even with a high-resolution computer screen, you'll have to use two displays: an NTSC-quality monitor next to the desktop PC to test the color and clarity of final DV images. This 14-inch Sony PVM14M4U Presentation Monitor is a video-industry staple, featuring Component YUV, Composite, and S-video inputs, as well as audio.

monitor, is used as a definitive reference for other video devices, which can drift out of adjustment. Calibrated to the proper ranges of color and luminance for broadcast TV, a reference monitor reveals hidden parts of the video signal and gives TV programmers a good look at the final product. For digital filmmakers, especially those creating images from scratch, a reference monitor can provide the first look at a digital file in the analog realm.

Unless you know that you're never going to want to show your movie on an analog device (which seems unlikely), you should seriously consider making a reference monitor a permanent addition to your production studio. Most models around the $1,500 price range are more than adequate for homes or small studios.

Here are a few things to look for when purchasing a reference monitor:

- **Screen size.** The size of a reference monitor is measured in diagonal inches, from the farthest corners of the cathode ray tube. If the monitor is to be a part of your desktop equipment, there's little need to get a huge screen because the distance between you and the monitor won't be significant. Don't place the monitor where it may pick up unwanted glare. If reflections are a problem, get a monitor with a flat screen rather than a rounded tube. Avoid a monitor less than 13 inches, because small tubes struggle to represent the flaws in details that may become obvious on larger sets. Reference monitors of less than 20 inches are the most popular, and they're also quite affordable.

- **Metal cabinet.** Monitors placed near electromagnetic equipment may interfere with the video signal and produce ghosted images or waving lines on the screen. If this interference is inevitable, consider a monitor with a metal cabinet to shield the signals.

- **Multiple inputs.** Make sure your monitor not only accepts professional component connections but also includes the S-video and composite analog jacks that are

(continued on page 82)

PREPARING RYB ARTWORK IN THE RGB WORLD

If you're a graphic designer creating still images or motion animation for television, you'll definitely want to use a reference monitor to check the quality of your work. Keep in mind that many television professionals joke that NTSC stands for *never the same color*. And indeed, you'll soon discover that even an expensive computer display or a top-shelf scan converter can't make the colors on your TV monitor look exactly the same as they do inside your software program.

Just like computer images, your NTSC reference monitor sees all pictures in an RGB format, separating the red, green, and blue information as separate signals. However, most artists and designers working with paint or printed inks must use the RYB palette, combining red, yellow, and blue to derive the full spectrum of color. (CMYK printing techniques are simply an extension of the RYB color system.) Imagine loading a client's logo onto a new Photoshop canvas, selecting the file for export over FireWire to your NTSC reference monitor, and sitting back in horror as you realize the colors cannot be accurately reproduced within the legal limits of broadcast TV. Even a computer-selected palette of NTSC-safe color swatches may at first sight look appealing but clash with adjoining colors when seen on a CRT—a phenomenon caused by the way the human eye reacts to phosphorous screen images, especially on cheap or older sets.

When designing title cards or motion graphics for television work, make sure you always use a reference monitor and stay away from the following problem areas:

- *Thin lines.* Using thin horizontal lines in your artwork will produce excessive flicker because the alternating interlaced fields of television can only display the line every other frame. Make sure your lines are at least several pixels wide. Even thin vertical or diagonal lines will appear to stair-step if they're not thick enough.

- *Small text.* For many of the same reasons, small text does not appear legible on television. Words that seem crisp and clear on a computer screen will be difficult to read under the lower-resolution line scans of standard TV sets.

- *Saturated colors.* Whenever possible, avoid using harsh, saturated colors directly adjacent to each other because these intense swatches (especially reds and greens) create shocking visual oscillations to the human eye. Grays and softer pastoral colors or earth tones (like the dusty tones found in the Westerns) tend to display quite well in NTSC.

ColorTheory lets you import almost any RYB artwork into a window so that you can find a harmonious match in TV's RGB world. By selecting a color in a frame of video, you can begin to use established color formulas to discover a pleasing complement.

A little-known killer app for designing broadcast images is ColorTheory DV. The digital equivalent of a color wheel, this application is being used by a growing number of TV and Web artists to transform the time-tested formulas for proper primary, secondary, tertiary, pastel, neutral, and discordant RYB schemes into the RGB color combinations that display well on reference monitors.

Working as a stand-alone application or as a plug-in for Photoshop and After Effects, ColorTheory allows you to import almost any artwork into a window so that you can scour through hundreds of tonal variations while viewing the original elements. Effectively, ColorTheory DV reconciles the variations of red, yellow, and blue with the quirks of NTSC/PAL monitors so that Web and broadcast designers can make their RGB work look as harmonious as traditional RYB masterpieces.

The color of the text in this image was found by selecting the blue pixels of the boat and asking ColorTheory to suggest a complementary color equivalent to one you might find on a traditional artist's color wheel.

In this scene, the controlled palette of colors in the footage would be ruined by harsh contrasts: Luckily, ColorTheory can recommend analogous colors that will achieve better results for the rolling titles.

common to home video equipment like DVD players and VCRs. This shouldn't be hard to find; most industrial reference monitors have composite inputs (although some use BNC-type connectors).

- **Degaussing switch.** Yep, even at home, errant magnetic fields can cause the colors of your reference monitor to shift. Make sure your monitor includes a Degauss button, which will demagnetize the screen. Some monitors automatically degauss every time they are turned on.

Reference monitors are calibrated to the television standards of a particular country. If you're creating movies for broadcast in the United States, you should use an NTSC reference monitor; if you're creating movies for broadcast in Europe, you should us a PAL reference monitor.

THE IMPORTANCE OF ALPHA CHANNELS

Television artwork is filled with traps. If you plan to create a lot of motion graphics for broadcast design, especially spinning logos and moving text, you should bone up on alpha channels—extra layers of information that travel with a file into video applications and help the software better integrate artwork into complex motion imagery. For a better understanding of alpha channels and their usefulness in preparing work for broadcast, consult a book on

motion graphics or title design. In addition, several videotape training series now offer excellent instruction on circumventing the pitfalls of TV graphics.

One of the finest resources for broadcast design is the Video Syncrasies videotape series. Hosted by broadcast designers Chris and Trish Meyer, the tapes explain the complexities of using alpha channels when compositing 3D art or EPS logos against moving backgrounds.

Scan Converters

If your modest budget prohibits the purchase of a reference monitor, you may be able to use a spare TV to gauge picture quality on analog devices. Scan converters, which turn your TV set into a large-screen computer display, bridge the technical divide between computer video displays and television sets by changing the electronic rate at which each monitor refreshes its images.

Computers can refresh images to the screen at a rate of up to 75,000 times a second, while TV sets move more slowly, drawing horizontal lines roughly 15,000 times per second. Scan converters modify the scanning speed of computer displays to make them compatible with TV displays. At the same time, scan converters can change the digital information of a DV stream into a composite analog signal for a standard television set.

While dozens of vendors offer the capable assistance of a scan converter, choosing one can be mind-boggling task. There are many kinds of scan converters to choose from. For example, if you're a mobile filmmaker, you might choose a portable scan converter to connect your laptop to any television set, providing an instant showcase of your work. But if you're creating

Focus Enhancements makes this high-end iTView DV scan converter specifically for the iMac DV models, which include a built-in VGA port (a 15-pin mini D-Sub connector) hidden in the rear of the housing. Instead of putting footage movies back out to the camcorder over FireWire, you can record DV movies or any on-screen action straight to a VCR.

software training videos, you might want to purchase a scan converter that records the onscreen actions of the computer mouse and file menus.

Another difficulty in choosing the right converter is that most of the ones on the market don't do a very good job. Many of the converters designed for simple multimedia presentations (like connecting a PC to a large TV at a trade show) don't follow the strict guidelines for video use: Some don't reconcile the interlace video images properly, causing an annoying flicker in images. And some converters can't handle the wide range of computer display resolutions and varying refresh rates, force-fitting your movie at odd sizes in the screen.

High-end scan converters, however, use a hardware chip technology to perform a direct pixel-to-pixel compression that prevents flicker, enhances small fonts, and fills the entire TV screen with a complete mirror image of your monitor. Some even handle resolutions of up to 1,600 by 1,280.

In choosing a scan converter, look for the following features:

- **NTSC and PAL.** Make sure the scan converter you purchase outputs a true NTSC (or PAL) signal, including composite video. Almost all scan converters provide this output as a standard feature. Because composite video is the lowest resolution possible, this often provides a gauge of the worst-case scenario for your picture quality.

- **24-bit color support.** Scan converters should be able to convert and output 24-bit color. However, be wary of advertising claims: Some scan converters can't handle 24-bit processing and subsequently downgrade images to 16-bit or less.

- **640 samples per line.** At minimum, look for scan converters that offer 640 samples per line. (And keep in mind that even this minimum sample rate often results in fuzzy pictures.) The more samples per line, the better the image quality.

- **Image manipulation.** Some scan converters allow you to manipulate the size and position of the incoming video signal if picture borders are not bleeding to the edges of

the screen. When showing movies on a TV monitor, this effect can pose problems. Likewise, if you're recording on-screen computer action (for training videos, etc.), the menu bars may be completely out of sight. Most converters compensate by "underscanning" to shrink the image both horizontally and vertically. Conversely, some converters offer overscanning controls that magnify or enlarge the picture to increase the readability of text or show significant details—even allowing you to zoom or pan.

- **Image freeze.** This helpful scan converter feature lets you select any image on screen as part of a paused playback and then ensures that it displays flicker-free on your TV screen until you instruct the system to continue.

Using Camcorders for Previewing

Still another way to check the look of DV footage on your TV set is to use the built-in circuitry of your digital camcorder. You can easily convert the video images traveling over a FireWire connection into analog signals by using the composite AV adapter cable included with most DV cameras: You simply use the camcorder as a go-between, taking pass-through playback from the computer and routing it through the camcorder to a nearby TV or VCR.

This solution is ideal for those who have only an occasional need to check the accuracy of their editing work on a television system.

Several utilities now exist, however, that let you use your camcorder preview capabilities for more than simply watching video playback. EchoFire, a simple control-panel application from Synthetic Aperture, sends still images from Adobe

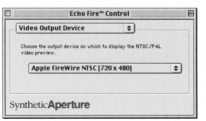

With EchoFire you can select the standard FireWire port on your computer to accept output from applications such as Photoshop and After Effects directly to your digital camcorder for preview.

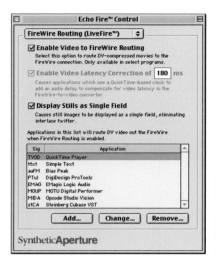

In addition to routing images to the camcorder, EchoFire can instantly stretch the aspect ratio of video to fit the screen or deinterlace still photos so that they don't flicker when displayed on a television set.

Photoshop and After Effects out through the FireWire connection in your computer, allowing you to preview artwork on any analog device connected to your camcorder. You can even use this utility to play movies straight from the QuickTime Movie Player to the handycam. This inexpensive application demonstrates the ways in which FireWire can facilitate project previews without requiring expensive hardware.

PREVIEWING AUDIO

Too often, digital video projects are undermined by poor recordings—the true sign of an amateur.

While reference monitors and TV sets can give you an accurate preview of your video, they are not a reliable way to listen to audio tracks. The built-in speakers on television sets can disguise the low-level vibrations that might become blaringly obvious on a sophisticated home theatre sound system.

Even if your RAM previews inside After Effects are set to display low-resolution feedback on the computer screen, EchoFire will send a full-quality rendered image to the FireWire port. If a camcorder or DV deck is connected to a reference monitor, EchoFire can even send DV clips directly to those devices from the QuickTime Movie Player.

PeakDV is a popular audio editing application used by professional sound designers. Although many video programs now feature audio tools, PeakDV goes a step further by offering true multitrack mixing capabilities and audio filtering.

SoftAcoustik rolled out the first FireWire-equipped speakers, which accept a 24-bit, 48K audio signal—straight out of a Macintosh FireWire port. This high-speed, high-bandwidth transfer allows greater 8-bit audio sampling—about 10 percent more aurreal information than contained in a typical CD-quality audio file.

So just as you should preview images on a reference monitor, you should also listen to your soundtrack on a reliable pair of reference speakers.

Audio monitors for computers have become commonplace, and an affordable pair of speakers (that provides better-than-multimedia sound but can't match that provided by your stereo system) is a smart investment. With a proper set of speakers, you can identify disturbing hums and hisses and remove them by using one of a number of shareware utilities.

Some professional audio applications go beyond the multi-track functionality of digital mixers and offer extended features for filmmakers. In many of these programs, you can preview a movie clip in a window as you listen to a selected track—helpful when choosing music for a scene or matching sound effects to an action. Other programs include special filters to remove the electronic noise created by the camcorder or other machines.

PREVIEWING UNCOMPRESSED FOOTAGE

At the highest end of digital movie production, editors use hardware-enhanced video playback devices to preview footage. The most common of these is a PCI card, slotted into the CPU and featuring a number of special chips that accelerate visual effects and boost overall performance. These supercharged PCI cards route video signals away from the computer's regular processor and assume control of video playback. Because these add-on cards have special algorithms wired into their circuitry, they can display transitions and certain rendered effects in real time. They can also handle the demands of playback for uncompressed video input, digital files recorded at a much higher data rate than standard DV camcorders can import.

In some cases, these cards act like superior scan converters, supporting higher-resolution workstations, refreshing the screen at faster rates, and offering better bit-rate processing of color (meaning that the converted images will feature more pixel depth than standard video compression).

Real Time vs. Rendered

Many of these expensive playback cards promise to eliminate rendering time for commonly used special effects in applications like Final Cut Pro. However, real time is a nebulous term. No computer system can render all effects with split-second response. Instead, these card manufacturers include hundreds of pre-set filters and effects that can be rushed to the display, making it seem as if you're working within an editing system with little delay between the time it takes to execute a command and the moment you see the results.

These special filters are accelerated by an additional processor chip included on the playback card. This chip is engineered to execute complex mathematical algorithms needed to perform the rendering at lightning speeds. Unlike your computer's processor, this chip is unencumbered with other tasks, and can dedicate all its power to completing its singular purpose—the quick playback of a few filter effects. The quick turnaround of these selected effects gives the computer user the impression that the clips are rendered instantly, or in real-time.

Realistically, though, most complex editing, effects and compositing options require more processing power than even the most professional-quality video playback card can supply. Thus, you're likely to encounter situations in which the computer can't effectively display all rendered effects in real time.

On standard systems (those without playback cards), you must simply wait for your software and the computer's central processor to complete the rendered effects before you can watch them on a reference monitor at normal speed.

Breakout Boxes

Some of the uncompressed video playback cards also include a breakout box, an interface board containing the necessary connectors for DV, component analog, D1, high-definition, and even 1080p/24 input and output. Component video—a popular format for encoding analog video sources that was developed for use in professional video production and recording—comes in several varieties, including Betacam and MII. Serial digital output, or D1, enables the breakout box to be used in conjunction with other digitally-based equipment in a broadcast environment.

The D1 Desktop 128HD capture/playback card from Digital Voodoo offers uncompressed support for HDTV video—which means you can edit and composite effects in film resolution in real time.

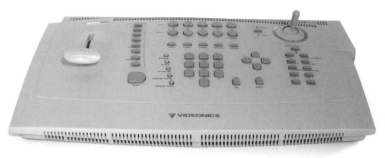

Not all real-time playback devices are PCI cards: The MXPro mixer from Videonics offers preprogrammed effects and transitions that can be applied to two incoming FireWire streams on the fly. Another FireWire port then outputs the combined images to the computer for capture.

Digital Displays

One day in the not-too-distant future, digital television will replace standard NTSC TV, offering ultrafine resolution programming like HDTV broadcasts. In addition, these monitors will replace our current computer monitors, allowing editors to output digital footage directly to noninterlaced, flicker-free tubes. These sets will possess more than twice the lines of resolution than the current NTSC picture, and will feature FireWire inputs for the fast delivery of high-resolution video.

Already, these digital televisions are available, and several flat-panel, all-digital monitors (like the SuperWide display from Silicon Graphics) currently deliver artifact-free MPEG video at 30 fps in the -1,600-by-1,024-pixel frame format.

The monitors also need hardware-enhanced playback cards, which are usually supplied with the purchase of the monitor. This emerging standard for displaying high-res digital signals will eventually complete the post-production environment for editors, removing the need to reference their playback on analog devices.

Bryan Boyce

Animator Bryan Boyce's *Special Report*, a crowd-pleasing short film, is a hilarious satire on the evening news that skewers just about every major figure in TV. Boyce captured footage of anchors Dan Rather, Ted Koppel, and Peter Jennings, and replaced their words with the melodramatic exclamations of B-movie actors in such retro science-fiction and horror film fare as *Plan 9 from Outer Space*, *Teenage Zombies*, and *Creature from the Black Lagoon*.

Boyce's first film, *Election Collectibles*, sparked great debate during the presidential campaign by using real footage of the candidates and inserting soundtracks of B-movie horror flicks to mock the media hype surrounding the candidates. Both *Special Report* and *Election Collectibles* have toured extensively with film festivals around the world, garnering plenty of laughter and praise along the way.

During production of these two films, Boyce got a lesson in converting analog video to digital files, and previewing the rendered effects on an NTSC monitor by outputting to a Media 100 playback card.

USING NEW MEDIA ON THE NEWS MEDIA

Animator Bryan Boyce imported clips of TV broadcasts into Adobe After Effects, and then removed their audio tracks. He captured the TV clips from an analog VCR but used a DV camcorder to record his friends lip-syncing the diabolical words of the B-movie actors. By creating a small matte around the mouths of the anchormen, Boyce supplanted footage of their lips into the new scene.

Although Boyce used digital video of his own mouth to speak the words of anchorman Brian Williams, he felt the composition looked too similar to the actual footage. So he added the devilish mustache and Van Dyke beard to draw attention to the effect. Using After Effects to composite the two video sources together, he was able to preview the rendered effects on an NTSC monitor by outputting to a Media 100 playback card.

At the climax of *Special Report*, the frantic warnings of news commentators reaches a peak when anchorwoman Connie Chung appears to be screaming at the top of her lungs to emphasize her costar's statement. The exaggerated mouth gives the celebrity a bizarre look when juxtaposed with her otherwise sedate expression.

Because many of the effects were so seamlessly integrated, Boyce had to create promotional stills with cartoon balloons to communicate the absurdity of the films in print.

chapter six

using still images

Many filmmakers know that when used thoughtfully, still photos provide a wonderful juxtaposition to moving images. Rather than use just video cameras, digital mediamakers *are able to combine DV cameras with digital still cameras, scanners, and printers to create work that's much more powerful than what they could produce using only one medium.*

A new line of FireWire-enabled digital still cameras and scanners is making it easy to add photos to movies.

Many animators produce movies with nothing but still images.

FireWire enhancements to digital still cameras have dramatically improved the speed at which image files can be transferred from camera to computer. And this in turn has allowed manufacturers to offer greater resolution and special preview features. In addition, FireWire lets the user control the camera remotely—a capability that's altered the use of this type of equipment in both commercial photography and filmmaking.

One wonderful application of these moviemaking tools is matte photography for special effects and virtual landscapes in 3D modeling. However, it's in the area of stop-motion animation that FireWire has truly revolutionized the field. In the past, animators had to have blind faith in the stop-motion process because each frame of their carefully crafted movies was exposed on a roll of film. Today, the guesswork is gone, giving animators a newfound freedom that is vividly expressed in the moving pictures they produce with nothing but still images.

While books on traditional filmmaking and editing seldom consider the use of still images, the desktop moviemakers of tomorrow are likely to have a rash of affordable and versatile FireWire cameras, scanners, and printers at their disposal.

HOW STILL PHOTOS ARE USED IN MOVIEMAKING

Incorporating still photos into motion pictures used to be a cumbersome process: Several complicated machines, like the optical printer and motion-control cameras, were employed to record multiple frames of the same photo onto celluloid. The operator would have to subtly move the plates holding a photograph to approximate the action of a camera zooming up for a close-up, smooth panning movements, or any other special effects.

In contrast, today's digital video programs like Apple Final Cut Pro and Adobe Premiere accept a wide variety of picture files. Once you've imported these images into your editing application, you can scale and rotate them with the click of a button. Most programs allow images in JPEG, PICT, BMP, GIF, and TIFF formats; a few even import Photoshop documents, retaining individual layers and effect properties.

Simple Storytelling via Still Photos

In the language of motion pictures, still photos can summon up an immediate, universal response without resorting to extraneous dialogue or narration—and they're inexpensive to use! For

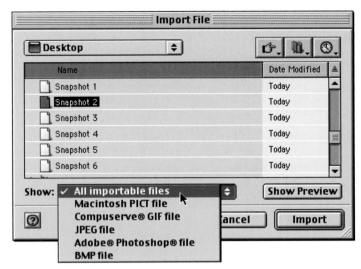

Most editing applications accept photographs in a number of picture formats. If your photos are not cropped to a 720-by-480 size and ratio, the software will reduce them to fit proportionally, leaving a black area around the edges of the frame.

this reason, advertisers often use pictures from stock-footage archives to lend credibility to their commercials without incurring the costs of actors, costumes, sets, and equipment.

The most common use of photos in movies has been for historical reference. Documentaries of Civil War battles, for example, rely heavily on archival photographs—mainly because they were all that was available at the time. In addition, still photographs can lend a sense of history and place the narrative in a specific period—which is why even modern movies introduce an assemblage of stills (often showing them as sepia-tone or black-and-white photos) when a character is reflecting on the past. A quick montage of images—usually accompanied by a monologue and ambient music—can compress a great deal of scope into just minutes of screen time.

Similarly, news reports often use still photos to visually support an interview or narration, drawing in on a portion of the photo to show informative content or emphasize a key point—a technique seen in crime thrillers where the detective will scan a newspaper article or love letter, suddenly zeroing in on a phrase that might have been overlooked initially.

This actress was photographed using two small DV cams just inches from each other. The result was footage that took the same line reading from two slightly different angles.

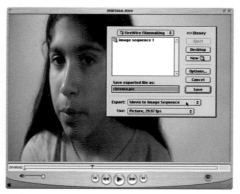

After capturing the clips from both cameras, the frames are converted to a sequence of still images using the Export feature in QuickTime Pro. A single audio track is exported from one of the clips.

When the sequences are imported into an editing program, every other frame of one sequence is substituted with a corresponding frame from the alternate angle. The final result is a stuttering shift in the picture, though the audio track keeps the actress in perfect sync throughout the scene.

When the subject of a movie is photography itself, as in the case in Michaelangelo Antonioni's classic suspense film *Blow Up*, the repetitive use of the same photo can create a sense of mystery, making viewers feel like they're missing a telling fact hiding in plain sight. Another innovative use of still images can be seen in Chris Marker's 1963 short film *La Jetee*, an experimental 30-minute science-fiction feature where still photos are used almost exclusively throughout the story, suggesting that the paranoiac images were merely fragments of the narrator's unreliable memory. Still photos can also become an enduring image at the conclusion of a film, like Francois Truffaut's *The 400 Blows*, where the protagonist is caught midair in a freeze frame, forever suspended at an emotional high point.

Creating Freeze Frames

You can easily create many still-image effects in your video-editing programs. In addition to importing a number of picture formats, most software applications allow you to isolate a single frame in your video footage and export it as a picture file for other uses.

When you convert video frames to still images, they retain the interlaced information of the original signal—a problem for designers who wish to print a movie still in a brochure or publish it on a Web page. Sometimes you'll see pixilated lines running through portions of the image—often during a freeze frame of swift action—or notice the still photos jittering when previewed on a reference monitor. You can easily remove this by applying a deinterlace filter in Photoshop, choosing to interpolate the missing field information.

Some applications automatically remove interlacing from still images, and some don't. For example, the original release of Apple's iMovie software created still images with interlaced information. When previewed on a reference monitor, these freeze frames vacillated between fields to produce a stutter. Version 2 of the same program fixed the problem, and now frames are saved without this troublesome jitter.

Exporting Image Sequences

Filmmakers wishing to promote their work often use time-lapse sequences to show a shot's individual frames. With most programs, these progressive images are easy to export: You simply export the movie clip as a picture sequence, and the computer generates as many images as there are frames in the clip. Be careful, though: You'll want to be sure to save a sequence to a specific folder because even a small clip can produce hundreds of files. If you unwittingly saved them to the wrong folder, you could have a jumbled mess on your hands.

Matte Photography and Special Effects

Photos are immeasurably useful in matte effects and chromakey work. Frequently, still images are used as false backdrops—that is, they're placed behind an actor removed from green-screen footage. They can also be added to parts of a composition to extend a scene's landscape. In fact, you've probably seen background vistas (skylines, buildings, sunsets) and foreground objects (fences, bushes, cars) in many contemporary movies that are actually nothing more than still photos used as simple mattes. Matte artists even "borrow" portions of a frame in one scene to conceal unwanted wires or objects that appear in the same sector of the frame, only later in sequence.

Instead of carting the cast and crew off to Hawaii for this effect, the actress was shot against a chromakey background, and a still image of a tropical sunset was used as the location. The image was slightly blurred and colorized to create the illusion of distance and to match the exposure of the video footage.

Stop-Motion Animation

Stop-motion photography—the first special-effect technique invented for the cinema—is a unique animation discipline that brings everyday objects to life by changing the position of elements over a period of time. Still pictures of a live-action set, usually populated by malleable models or figurines with armatures, are taken individually and then played together in a sequence at film speeds to show motion.

Pioneered by animators Willis O'Brien and Ray Harryhausen in films like *King Kong* and *The Seventh Voyage of Sinbad,* stop-motion effects were once the exclusive domain of science-fiction and horror films. Today, however, this well-established cinematic technique can be seen in commercials featuring puppets as product spokesmen—the Pillsbury Doughboy or the California Raisins—who seem to move of their own volition. And some filmmakers prefer the style it lends to their movies. The success of recent productions like Tim Burton's *The Nightmare Before Christmas,* and *James and the Giant Peach* proves the technique remains popular with audiences. In fact, many films provide a clever mix of full-size puppets, computer-generated graphics, and traditional stop-motion animation. *Jurassic Park* is an excellent example.

In the past, many stop-motion animators achieved their effects by integrating miniature creatures with live-action footage, or by building elaborate sets. For scenes in which humans were present, rear projection screens were often used to matte the animated characters into each frame of the movie. These days, however, it's cheaper and faster to use software programs to composite animated figures into live-action scenes. The computer can also blend frames to simulate the in-between movement normally associated with filmed actions—overcoming a major limitation of the stop-motion method, which appears stiff without any blur in still images.

However, computer technology (specifically FireWire) has also added new versatility to older stop-motion methods. For example, you can now connect a DV camcorder directly to the

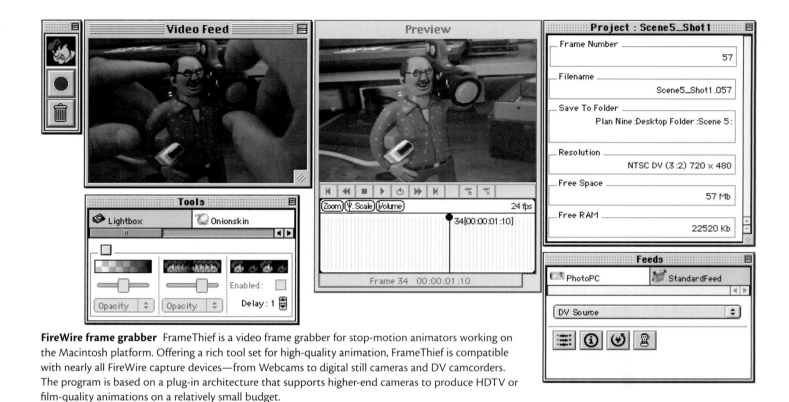

FireWire frame grabber FrameThief is a video frame grabber for stop-motion animators working on the Macintosh platform. Offering a rich tool set for high-quality animation, FrameThief is compatible with nearly all FireWire capture devices—from Webcams to digital still cameras and DV camcorders. The program is based on a plug-in architecture that supports higher-end cameras to produce HDTV or film-quality animations on a relatively small budget.

FireWire port on your computer and use video frame grabber programs like FrameThief to capture frames one at a time. FireWire-equipped digital still cameras also work in these applications, which can import pictures immediately, allowing you to review them in loop cycles, and reject them for better images. Previously, animators had to guess if the filmed exposure had recorded the movement accurately. Today, they can preview each frame and make subtle adjustments before capturing the final image.

There are, however, some problem areas when using DV cameras for still-image photography, especially in stop-motion work. If you're using a digital camcorder, make sure you lock the automatic exposure and manual white balance settings to prevent the camera from making adjustments that can change the lighting and introduce tiny fluctuations from

frame to frame. Because stop-motion work relies heavily on the "persistence of vision"—a phenomenon of the human brain that makes a rapid sequence of independent images appear as fluid motion—to create the illusion of movement, any changes in the variables of your subject, set, lighting, or camera will reveal shifting details in the final sequence and spoil the magic. The automatic features contained in DV camcorders can be very detrimental to this process.

FireWire-Equipped Still Cameras

Although digital cameras have been around for several years, FireWire technology has expanded their use and capabilities. By speeding the transport of images to computers,

FireWire has encouraged manufacturers to experiment with ultra-high-resolution sensors that create jumbo data files previously unheard of in small cameras. FireWire's ability to preview and transfer images in real time means that digital still cameras can better serve the fields of stop-motion and time-lapse photography.

Digital still cameras allow you to capture high-quality still images and transfer them to your system without developing pictures or reloading film canisters. Because FireWire-based cameras offer greater speed, digital pictures taken with them generally are larger file sizes. The latest models, in fact, are pushing the limits of photo resolution beyond 6 million pixels with every shutter click.

The highly anticipated Nikon D1 signaled the future of high-quality digital still imaging. Animators immediately picked up on FireWire-enabled cameras' ability to hook up to computers and control photo capture directly using Nikon's optional software—ideal for stop-motion animation.

Better still, many of these cameras use FireWire connections to talk to computer programs and adjust the exposure and color of pictures *before* they're snapped—a radical change from digital photography of the past, when people thought the only way to manipulate photos was to alter them in software *after* they had been taken. Future models of such cameras will coordinate with programs like Photoshop to track corrections made to preview images so that they can adjust their optics and exposure settings before final capture.

DOWNLOADING DIGITAL PHOTOS

FireWire has proved a boon to digital photographers, who had been looking for a fast way to get their large photo files into computers. Early-model digital cameras stored their images on internal hard drives and employed slow mechanisms—serial cable connections, parallel port card readers, infrared, USB cables, and PCMCIA adapters—built into their housings to offload the pictures. However, all of these interface types were inherently sluggish when transferring massive image files, and all became immediately obsolete when Flash memory was adopted as a photo standard. Flash memory cards hold images on removable RAM cartridges, which can then be placed into a card reader and copied to the hard drive of your computer. When camera maker Nikon began producing FireWire-equipped still cameras, the combination of swappable Flash memory and an ultrafast interface made its D1 model a much-sought-after piece of equipment. Even makers of Flash memory card readers began incorporating FireWire connectors to speed the transfer of images to the computer.

While Flash memory made it convenient for digital photographers to take their cameras on long trips, piling up collections of photos by simply swapping out memory cards, FireWire opened up several options for downloading images from the camera. Because FireWire cables can shuffle images to a computer for preview, many photographers save memory space by examining their photos before downloading them. Those that don't make the grade are deleted from the memory cards before they reach the computer's hard drive. FireWire can also capture photos from still

This FireWire compact flash card reader is a plug-and-play device designed to facilitate the high-speed transfer of photos from removable memory cards into the computer. Compatible with all operating systems, the reader accepts media from any Type I/II compact Flash card in increments of 16MB, 32MB, 64MB, 80MB, and 160MB, as well as IBM Microdrive cartridges.

The Foveon II still camera represents the standard in high-res digital photography. A built-in FireWire connection means this stand-alone camera can be connected to a host PC or Windows notebook (using supplied software) so that photographers can use a laptop screen as a line-of-sight viewfinder. High-speed FireWire outputs also let you capture one 2,048-by-2,048 image every second.

cameras at the same time it records the image on a Flash memory card. Perhaps best of all, FireWire cameras can be controlled by computer software, which means that still images can be captured and transferred from within moviemaking applications.

Many filmmakers, particularly animators, like to preview still images in a line-of-sight configuration. Line-of-sight means the animator, for example, can place a digital still camera in front of a small laptop and send computer instructions over FireWire to the camera. They can then preview precise frames and capture or reject them at will. FireWire-equipped line-of-sight cameras are also finding favor with commercial photographers who like being able to communicate face-to-face with their subjects as they preview images.

Checking for Resolution

Nearly all digital still cameras record images at much higher resolutions than DV footage. Some exceptional cameras can even take color information that rivals the best film formats. It's common today to get resolutions of more than 2 million pixels (or megapixels) in every photo you shoot. However, most individual frames of DV footage contain only 1.1 megapixels of data. This means that some of the information in your images will be discarded when the photos are incorporated into your editing programs and compressed as a digital video stream. If you plan to use zooming effects on still photographs (as seen in documentaries like Ken Burns' popular PBS series *The Civil War*), you may want to retain the highest resolution possible because images can lose valuable resolution as they are enlarged in the frame.

If you plan to use still images for multiple projects, it's best to save them in a lossless photo format like TIFF or PSD once you've transferred them from your camera. Most cameras compress photos as JPEG files; however, if you continuously open and save the same image as a JPEG-compressed image, the file will progressively lose pixel and color information. If your editing application only accepts GIF or JPEG formats, try to work in a lossless format until you've finished manipulating your photographs, then save a copy of the file to the required formats for video editing. Likewise, if you plan to print your images at photo quality, you'll want to retain the highest resolution possible.

Several miniature and specialty cameras capture digital photos that are well below the quality of standard video. Still photographs taken with surveillance equipment or wristwatch cameras, for example, come in well under the megapixel threshold for clear video. Although there's nothing wrong with using low-resolution images for moviemaking—some of the most innovative entries in recent film festivals have been made with stills from photocopiers, screen captures, and kiddy cameras—you should be aware that importing such images into your editing application will likely involve a process of interpolation. The software will have to compensate for the missing pixel data when it blows up the image to DV standards.

Many programs won't allow you to incorporate super-low-resolution images like Web graphics or thumbnails. Others will simply import the stills at their original size and provide a black band around the image to fill in the missing pixel data. If you're cropping images in Photoshop before importing them into an editing program, make sure you use proportions that are consistent with your final movie (most DV films use an aspect ratio of 4:3 when displayed).

Square and Nonsquare Pixels

Because most computers create images that consist of square pixels, the majority of animations and pictures you design from scratch (that is, any digitally created artwork other than photographs) will have a square-pixel aspect ratio. However, DV footage is captured and displayed in a nonsquare-pixel aspect ratio, an inequity that can cause photos to become distorted when imported in editing programs. Applications like Adobe After Effects will create layer elements and solids that have the same pixel aspect ratio as their source footage. For example, most of the masks and effects in a composition will honor the pixel aspect ratio of the original layer.

However, if you create pictures in Photoshop, you'll invariably make square-pixel images. Many artists assume that a dimension of 720 by 480 pixels will match their frame size of NTSC DV video; however, the difference in pixel aspect ratios means that the software must either crop the sides or scale your image to make the square-pixel picture fit perfectly in your nonsquare-pixel composition.

To avoid having your images cropped or stretched, create your Photoshop files at 720 by 534. Then, once you've imported the file into most editing programs, the still image will mix perfectly with video footage. In After Effects, you can simply use the Shrink to Fit command after importing the picture into the composition.

Some people prefer to create square-pixel still images at 640-by-480 resolution before incorporating them with DV footage in a composition because their digital camera includes automatic settings for photos at this size. However, this technique forces the application to interpolate data, producing a slight loss of resolution. Although the effects often are indistinguishable, sometimes this process can result in a pixilated look as the bitmapped images are scaled to more than 100 percent of their original size.

Conversely, some applications (for example, many DVD authoring programs) require that images be imported at 640-by-480 resolution, and subsequently stretch them to match the DV composition. This can be frustrating when you're designing interactive menus or preparing still images for DVD. One trick you can use to compensate for the photograph's distortion is to squish 720-by-480 pictures into a 640-by-480 canvas (using the Image Size command in Photoshop) before saving the file. This way, menus and still photographs will look proportionate when stretched to the DV aspect ratio by the authoring software.

If you don't need to fit the picture exactly into the frame size, you can simply create square-pixel images in Photoshop, and scale your images in an After Effects composition. If the picture doesn't look like it will match the resolution of DV footage, don't worry: After Effects will interpret all pixel aspect ratio information correctly when it outputs the final file.

SCANNERS AND PRINTERS

FireWire's widespread adoption on the graphics-intensive Macintosh platforms enabled manufacturers to justify putting the fast IEEE-1394 inputs on a new generation of scanners and printers. The device makers have capitalized on the technology by allowing artists to scan photos not just at greater speeds but at better color density and resolution. FireWire advancements mean that pictures can be scanned in a single pass—without interpolation. These advancements have also resulted in dramatically improved dot-per-inch (DPI) parameters for image scanning: Today's flatbed models can easily handle 9,600-by-9600 resolutions.

Naturally, the performance of these FireWire scanners makes them an excellent addition to graphic arts studios, photography labs, and pre-press environments. And because most of these scanners are also cross-platform compatible, they're also popular in corporate settings where equipment is shared among workgroups.

Surprisingly, some filmmakers pay more attention to scanners than they do to camcorders. In the last several years, a slew of avant-garde artists have made exceptional movies from scanned images—never using a video camera to produce motion footage. These films, like Rodney Ascher's short *Somebody Goofed,* have delighted film festival audiences using nothing more than pages from comic books or religious pamphlets that have been animated to move in ways that emulate the story structure of movies. In another Ascher short, *Budda Bar,* a series of prints from a cheap disposable camera were developed at a drive-through lab, scanned into a computer, manipulated in After Effects, and set to music. The result is a fluid mix of real locations with cut-out characters drifting through photo-realistic backgrounds.

Scanned photographs can also serve as texture maps for 3D animators trying to create a natural look in virtual

environments. For example, since it's nearly impossible to get your hands on a WWII tank for shooting a low-budget epic, many artists will scan pictures of aircraft or military equipment, tracing points in the photos for modeling data and wrapping the images around three-dimensional objects to simulate the look of the original.

Printers represent the last class of devices to take advantage of FireWire technology—in part because of the number of driver standards and interface requirements spawned by thousands of manufacturers over the last few decades. Still, FireWire printers do exist, and many more models are expected (particularly among higher-end printers) as graphic artists and photographers come to look for the responsiveness of their other FireWire peripherals in their printers. While USB printers have long been the economical choice for home users, FireWire printers will undoubtedly appeal to professionals because of their ability to handle higher-resolution data: By supporting increased file sizes, FireWire printers can produce high-quality color photos that at first glance are often indistinguishable from traditional photos.

In addition, FireWire printers can greatly improve productivity when they're directly connected to computers because they aren't affected by the slowdown of traffic over regular network bandwidth. They also function extremely well as shared printers for small workgroups on Fibre-channel or FireWire networks.

Twice as fast as a SCSI scanner, the Astra 6400 printer from UMAX can handle 60-by-1,200-dpi images at 42-bit resolution because of its ultrafast interface. An intelligent processor built into the scanner automatically detects whether a photograph should be rendered in color, grayscale, or black and white, and auto-crops the image area.

The Epson Stylus Color 900G was the first printer to support FireWire connectivity—and immediately boasted the fastest performance of any four-color ink-jet printer in its class. This blazing model prints up to 12 pages per minute.

Mark Osborne

Filmmakers like Mark Osborne are a dying breed. This patient graduate of the California Institute of the Arts practices the painstaking craft of stop-motion animation. His persistence has paid off: Osborne's masterwork in the stop-motion form, *More*, was nominated for an Academy Award in 1998.

Reaching beyond conventional filmmaking to achieve a unique look, Osborne has made his mark by incorporating computer processes into his working methods as he creates mixed-media forms. For his latest project, Osborne used a FireWire-enabled still camera to integrate stop-motion cutouts with photo-realistic backgrounds. The digital short, *Darwin Weeps*, features tiny sets built from digital stills that are output to a high-quality dye-sublimation printer and then mounted to pliable foam core. As Osborne was shooting, he used a motion-control camera to create 3D effects.

Darwin Weeps marks a milestone for Osborne and animators like him, demonstrating that old-school methods still have a place in an industry marching toward an all-digital future.

A MOVING EXPERIENCE WITH STILL IMAGES

Using a Nikon D1 camera for his short *Darwin Weeps*, animator Mark Osborne snapped more than 1,000 digital still images of his actors in different positions. After printing these photos to an Epson 980 printer, he mounted the 4-by-6 prints on foam core and created hundreds of character cutouts.

The background of this scene is a three-dimensional set comprised of 8-by-10 prints. Although the sets first appear to be flat and seamlessly integrated with the characters, their depth is revealed by movement of the camera mounted to a motion-control device. Osbourne also uses compositing filters in After Effects to give a pixilated look to his characters' faces.

Placing the character into a movie theater meant creating dozens of seats in descending sizes. It's hard work, but the effect pays off when the interplay of light and shadows reveals the details of the set. Osborne carefully moves the limbs and torsos, and replaces the heads with one of 500 expressions, before taking a snapshot and importing the digital photo into Adobe Premiere. By running the stills through a looping sequence, he can accept or reject the image and reset the characters for the next shot.

chapter seven

setting up a network

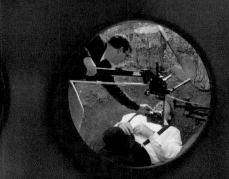

Historically, video artists have been slow to embrace collabo-
ration because it hasn't been easy to exchange footage or
work simultaneously on the same project. File-compression
technologies represented a giant leap toward giving multiple
editors or designers access to the same source footage.
And more recently, FireWire-facilitated developments in
networking technologies have
made it feasible to centralize
project files and decentralize the
individuals who access them—liberating the
filmmaking process.

FireWire networks are increasingly popular with small workgroups.

Suddenly, the lone director can farm out parts of his or her
project—over the network—to get help in areas where special skills or knowledge are required. An editor can work on
the rough cut of a movie while a digital artist is rendering
special effects to the same source footage. In these cases,
each individual is accessing the same file from a network
server, which then synchronizes the changes and streams
back the latest version of the project in real time.

Likewise, as corporations, advertising agencies, and graphic
arts studios begin collaborating on digital video projects, the
number of companies sharing footage continues to grow.
Many shops are using special high-capacity FireWire storage
devices and DVD-RAM-based systems to create storage area
networks (SANs)—powerful networks that allow multiple
users to access the same file for color correction, special
effects, or simple editing without duplicating or disrupting
the original source footage.

FireWire networks are also proving to be increasingly popular among consumers and smaller workgroups, who seek their simplification and affordability. Consumers can easily inter-connect two FireWire-enabled computers for immediate file sharing, and small workgroups can access printers and storage servers over simple network configurations using nothing more than a few FireWire cables.

Unfortunately, detailing the precise steps in setting up a FireWire network is beyond the scope of this chapter. But filmmakers should understand the basic networking capa-bilities that lay dormant in their FireWire cables, and the immense opportunities that await individuals who seek to link their computers and devices to others around the home or the office.

SUPERIOR NETWORK SPEED

Many of the same reasons FireWire has been incorporated into a large range of peripherals and devices make it ideal for con-necting computers as well. Here are just a few of the benefits:

- FireWire operates at between 100 Mbps and 400 Mbps— up to four times faster than the even the previous offer-ings in digital video environments. Network applications have already shown that they can provide exceptional performance levels for moving video files in professional broadcast facilities—even exceeding the speed and func-tionality of Ethernet and Fibre Channel solutions.

- FireWire operates at isochronous data transfer levels, which means it can stream video with very little latency—even while it's sending traditional data over the same cables.

- FireWire links workstations, servers, printers, and storage devices without the need for termination. And these FireWire devices are hot-pluggable and eliminate the need to set the ID switches.

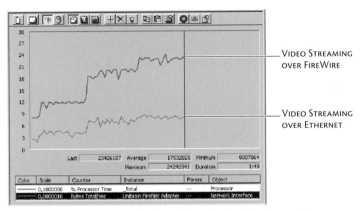

VIDEO STREAMING OVER FIREWIRE

VIDEO STREAMING OVER ETHERNET

Exceeding Ethernet These benchmark results clearly illustrate the superiority of FireWire over 100-Mbps Ethernet. Tested under a dual-boot operating system designed for IEEE-1394 networking (like the Windows 2000 configuration shown here), FireWire reaches nearly 200-Mbps performance, doubling the speed of its competitor.

- With FireWire, each computer can operate independently of a central controlling server, yet they all accept com-mands from any other linked device.

- Multiple computers can be connected to the same FireWire bus without using crossover cables or special adapters

SIMPLE FILE-SHARING CONFIGURATIONS

Not all filmmakers need to collaborate over elaborate net-works—some only need to transfer files between a small num-ber of computers. FireWire is of enormous benefit for this use. A FireWire cable lets you transfer massive files from your lap-top to your desktop in minutes. And in most cases, two PCs with FireWire adapters need no other hardware to begin net-working immediately.

Already, most operating systems (Windows 98, Windows 2000, Macintosh, and Linux) include some level of FireWire net-working support. And even consumer electronics products like Sony's PlayStation 2 include built-in FireWire ports so that they will be ready to connect to the next generation of networkable games and programming delivered over televisions, set-top boxes, and the Internet.

SHARING FIREWIRE PERIPHERALS
ALTHOUGH MULTIPLE COMPUTERS CAN SHARE DATA OVER FIREWIRE, NOT ALL OPERATING SYSTEMS LET YOU SHARE PERIPHERALS. WHEN MORE THAN ONE COMPUTER IS CONNECTED TO A FIREWIRE PERIPHERAL SUCH AS A HARD DRIVE OR CD-ROM DRIVE, THE FIRST COMPUTER THAT'S TURNED ON CONTROLS THE DEVICE.

Target Disk Mode

One of the easiest ways to connect two computers and begin sharing files is with a simple system configuration called *target disk mode*. Although this feature is currently only available on Macintosh computers, target disk mode theoretically allows any computer with a FireWire port (the target computer) to be used as an external hard disk. The target computer appears as a hard disk icon on the desktop of another computer—the host computer. Thus, you could use your G4 workstation to mount your PowerBook G3 as an additional volume—like a portable hard disk—which can be accessed with full read/write permission, just like any other storage device. Target disk mode will work on any FireWire-equipped PowerBook, iBook, Power Mac G4, G4 Cube, or iMac with Firmware version 2.4, FireWire 2.3.3 drivers, and Mac OS 8.6 or later installed.

Target disk mode isn't a true networking configuration, because only one computer remains fully operational; however, it does provide a handy way for a single user to quickly connect two computers and transfer files between internal hard disks. For Macintosh users, this feature can be an indispensable tool in the moviemaking process.

Booting a Target Computer

To successfully execute this operation, be sure that your target computer is shut down and that you've removed all other FireWire devices from both computers prior to activating target disk mode. Although you don't need to turn off the host computer, you must connect both computers with six-pin-to-six-pin cables before starting. Apple also recommends that you connect the computers to AC power.

As you boot up the target computer, press down the *T* key until the monitor displays the FireWire logo. Once the target computer is up and running, its internal hard disk will appear as an icon on the Finder of the host computer. Now you're ready to copy files to or from that volume. Note that peripherals attached to a target computer will not be accessible by the host computer.

When you've finished transferring files, you can simply drag the target computer's icon to the Trash (or select Put Away from the File menu) and disconnect the six-pin FireWire cable. Don't attempt to reconnect any FireWire devices until you've disconnected the two computers from each other or stopped using target disk mode. Finally, if you unplug the

A quick way to connect two Macintosh computers is by using *target disk mode*—a feature of the Mac OS that lets a host computer mount the internal hard drive of another FireWire computer simply by using a six-pin cable.

target computer and then try to reconnect it to the host, you may find that the hard disk icon doesn't appear on the host desktop. In this case, just check the cable connections and restart the host computer.

Connecting Multiple Computers

In a perfect world, you would only have to plug a dozen FireWire computers together to have them intelligently configure themselves into a functional network within seconds. Although that day is coming, it's not here yet—which means you can't just slap some FireWire cable between multiple machines and start sharing files.

However, there are ways to make your operating system work over third-party FireWire networking programs. Many of these solutions operate expertly across mixed computing environments, communicating easily between Macs and PCs. While you won't always reach peak data rates of 400 Mbps, you can expect to get 200 Mbps regularly, and if you're already accustomed to moving large video files over your office network, FireWire data transfer will seem lightning-fast.

In many workgroups, updating a network to include FireWire (or building an exclusively FireWire-based network) will likely entail purchasing add-on cards for older computers, printers, and network storage devices. Several manufacturers now sell complete FireWire networking kits, designed to provide all the necessary hardware and software to connect cross-platform servers and systems over FireWire.

FireNet Networking Software

Unless you're using Microsoft's Windows ME operating system, you'll likely need special software if you want a fully functional FireWire network. Currently, only Windows ME can automatically configure computers connected by FireWire into an instant network. Thankfully, FireWire networking software is available for both Windows 2000 and Macintosh users. One company, Unibrain, manufactures Ethernet emulation software called FireNet, which routes IP data over FireWire for networking in PC-to-PC, Mac-to-Mac, or PC-to-Mac

If you need to bring older computers and laptops up to FireWire standards, manufacturer UniBrain packages FireWire Networking Kits, complete with PCI or PCM/CIA cards, cabling, and the company's special FireNet software.

> **WINDOWS ME SUPPORT**
> CURRENTLY, WINDOWS ME IS THE ONLY OPERATING SYSTEM THAT INCLUDES NATIVE SUPPORT FOR FIREWIRE NETWORKING. AFTER INSTALLING A FIREWIRE CARD IN A WINDOWS ME COMPUTER, A VIRTUAL "NETWORK ADAPTER" IS ACTIVATED IN NETWORK PROPERTIES AND WILL AUTOMATICALLY CREATE ITS OWN IP CONFIGURATION FOR THE NETWORK.

configurations. Unibrain also makes a version for Macintosh computers, optimized for Mac OS 9 with Appleshare IP or Mac OS X.

Although FireNet is not nearly robust enough to handle the daily networking demands of a television studio, it's ideal for clusters of computers dedicated to desktop video projects. For small groups of DV moviemakers, FireNet provides a smart way of squeezing extra performance out of the already existing bandwidth in their FireWire cables. FireNet is extremely simple to set up and more affordable than traditional networking software. A trial version is available on the FireWire Filmmaking DVD-ROM

FireNet can perform at speeds four times faster than Fast Ethernet by using pure TCP/IP. After installing FireNet, all data (not just audio, video, and graphics files) moves along the six-pin cables. Because FireNet has much greater data capacity than Fast Ethernet systems, you can connect more clients to a network before it becomes saturated. In tests of several Macs connected with TCP/IP over a FireWire network, FireNet software was able to simultaneously stream six DV files from the same server before the network began to slow down or show signs of sluggishness.

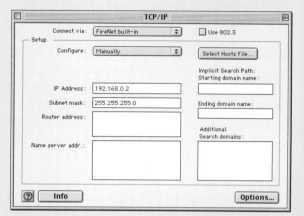
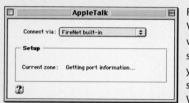
File-Sharing Devices

Near-line storage devices represent another way of sharing files, without using complex networking software. As its name suggests, near-line storage doesn't take the form of an internal disk, nor does it attach to a large server. Rather, it's usually a single device that provides access to data that has been backed up onto removable or restorable media.

The latest incarnation of near-line storage is the CD or DVD jukebox, an enclosure holding discs that can be stored in groups within magazines or held in a main carousel. By burning digital assets onto CDs and DVDs, filmmakers can make reusable-media files accessible at all times. These jukeboxes are ideal for individuals or small collectives of filmmakers who need to keep large libraries of commonly used photos, sound effects, logos, and movie clips archived in one place.

At the high end of the professional market, a jukebox (which resembles a large storage cabinet) can hold as many as 1,000 DVD discs and perform fast enough to serve a vast library of digital movies to hundreds of users on demand. Many of the units come preinstalled with digital-media management software used to catalog files through a Web browser or visual search system.

Although these devices give users the ability only to read and copy files from optical media, they're extremely cost-effective and flexible. The discs are relatively inexpensive; CD-R burners are reasonably priced; digital assets are saved in an immutable form; and the discs can be easily shuffled when the collection needs to be updated.

These jukeboxes from PowerFile hold up to 200 digital discs in a networkable FireWire device and easily attach to an existing Macintosh or PC file-sharing system to give workgroups fast and simultaneous access to DVDs and CD-ROMs.

Building Larger Networks

If your production environment requires that you stream full DV clips from a centralized server, you may need to consider a more robust network configuration. Television studios, broadcast design studios, and special effects houses often struggle to implement networks fast enough to sustain the proper throughput that video requires to stream without interruptions.

Thankfully, the underlying technology of FireWire networks does an exceptional job of addressing these concerns. Furthermore, networks based on FireWire can speed the transfer of massive media files when backing up workstations and servers.

Dynamic Network Factory's FireFly 1000 is an ideal network backup solution device that mirrors data to two removable hard drives simultaneously, intelligently recovering data in the event of server or system crashes. If one drive fails, the FireFly 1000 will automatically rebuild the data to the new drive.

Protocol Options

Before the advent of FireWire, most broadcast facilities adopted some variation of ATM, Ethernet, or Fibre Channel for their network configurations. By today's standards, many of these protocols are too slow and expensive to enable multiple users to stream audio and video across networks, or to access storage for archiving and backing up. In most cases, FireWire has bypassed many of their shortcomings altogether. But because these solutions are still available, it's important to distinguish them from one another.

Before choosing a protocol to move video across your network, you should understand the options available to you.

Asynchronous Transfer Mode

ATM is a high-speed cell-switching transport standard once favored for audio work but now nearly incapable of providing reliable, speedy delivery of large files. Designed to handle both data and voice traffic over low-bandwidth networks such as Internet infrastructures and telephone networks, ATM was once used by broadcast networks for video applications. Today, however, the standard has lost favor with many broadcasters because it no longer integrates easily with state-of-the-art equipment.

Ethernet

This inexpensive protocol is used extensively in both general computing environments and broadcast facilities, primarily for local application and file sharing. However, while standard 10Base-T and 100Base-T Ethernet networks work just fine for most scheduling systems and central media databases, this type of network is rarely used for transferring video files.

Another version of Ethernet technology, called Fast Ethernet (or Gigabit Ethernet), uses standard Ethernet interfaces (so that it fits neatly into existing networks) but gets improved performance from fiber-optic connections. The increased bandwidth makes this type of Ethernet a popular choice for high-speed video transfer; however, the technology is still relatively new, and most broadcasters and studios have only implemented Fast Ethernet to interconnect video servers.

Fibre Channel

This is the latest buzz among video facilities because it provides both fast connections (between 600 Mbps and 1 Gbps) and intelligent switches that make video delivery extremely reliable. Unfortunately, most Fibre Channel protocols are still proprietary—which means this is not only an expensive solution but one that typically doesn't coexist with other network devices. For these reasons, most Fibre Channel networks are installed as part of a comprehensive solution, featuring a single manufacturer's entire product family.

Unfortunately, ATM, Fast Ethernet, and Fibre Channel networks can only transport video as *asynchronous* data, which means that digital files must pass through some other interface (usually SDI for video) during delivery, and are therefore subject to interruptions or loss of bandwidth. Because of this, precise timing cannot be guaranteed. In broadcast environments, this can mean a change in the synchronization of audio and video or a slip in timecode—a recipe for disaster.

Isochronous Data over FireWire

Unlike most computer network protocols (which were designed to handle data), FireWire was developed to route video content *and* data in asynchronous and *isochronous* ways. Isochronous data transport provides a fixed channel on the network for *guaranteed* delivery of video streams. As a result, the network must allocate a portion of its bandwidth to ensure that isochronous data streams are never interrupted or reduced in signal strength—regardless of other network traffic. In addition to connecting digital camcorders, this feature makes FireWire an extremely good networking technology for use in video-intensive environments.

Designed to carry multimedia, control information, and data, FireWire offers isochronous service for high-bandwidth streams (like video) and asynchronous service for low-bandwidth packets (like simple instructions). Another attractive capability of FireWire technology is its support of up to 64 individual isochronous channels on a link. This means multiple streams of full-frame video can be carried simultaneously on a single cable. Better yet, FireWire sets aside a fixed amount (80 percent) of its capacity for video—which means that regardless of network traffic, a video stream can immediately travel over the cable without any latency.

Even if Ethernet and Fibre Channel networks were able to transport isochronous data, they would still have another hurdle to overcome: These protocols allow for different formats of asynchronous data, which means they require a multitude of connections when getting video into and out of a server. FireWire circumvents this problem by carrying all of the isochronous and asynchronous information on the same cable—benefits that make FireWire an unrivaled networking standard for video editing.

Choosing a Network Configuration

Once you've decided which network protocol is best suited to delivering multimedia across your work environment, you need to determine how to configure it. Basically, you've got three options: storage area networks (SANs), networked attached storage (NAS), or video area networks. While SAN configurations involve fairly sophisticated integration with a server, NAS devices are considerably simpler, offering smaller workgroups an easy way of adding functionality to an existing network with much complexity. Video area networks, on the other hand, are high-end implementations for professional production facilities.

Storage Area Networks

Over the past several years, SAN configurations have captivated media artists. SANs are essentially centralized storage devices connected to ultrafast servers used for one purpose—speeding

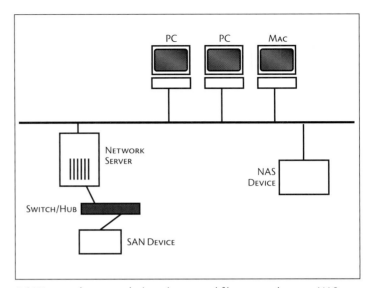

A SAN controls storage devices via a central file server, whereas a NAS device is attached directly to the network and works independently of the network server, delivering files directly to workstations. Both SAN and NAS devices can coexist on the same network.

large file transactions. Thus, any device connected to a SAN will zip video and data files to any connected workstation from a central data repository. In studio environments, the SAN aims to make video footage available to all users all the time. Currently, Fibre Channel is the most common implementation in SAN environments, but lately several FireWire devices have found favor among DV producers.

SANs are often difficult to install and maintain because to control access to the shared volumes, you must use complex, proprietary network management software. To route data between workstations and storage devices, many SANs incorporate a switcher, which can be a separate piece of hardware attached to the network server. And in many implementations (even in FireWire SANs), you must install software drivers that run on every workstation or configure an external workstation to synchronize access to all stored material. In addition, any devices that you plan to attach to the SAN must be able to work with this proprietary software, limiting network access to workstations only.

This 600GB NAS device contains its own file management software, a trimmed-down operating system designed to speed files to workstations.

That said, the SAN concept is a sound one, and—ultimately—it may be the way most large production companies collaborate on video projects. For smaller studios, however, network attached storage, or NAS, may provide an alternative to SANs.

Network Attached Storage

A NAS device provides a much simpler way of adding additional storage to a FireWire network. Designed to bypass the I/O bottleneck of a network server and boost performance by delivering files directly to the requesting workstation, NAS devices are best suited for file serving (like video streams). In contrast, SAN devices are best suited to handling large volumes of block data such as database applications.

Whereas SAN drives depend on instructions from the network file server to deliver data (and a switcher to route data), NAS drives contain their own file system software—sort of like a mini operating system, free of the clutter required to run an entire network and stripped down to just the software needed to serve files directly to workstations. Although NAS devices are technically servers, they act more like intelligent hard drives. They can be easily configured to work on hard disks, optical disks, and tape backup systems, and attach directly to any point on a LAN. In most cases, NAS devices provide an excellent source of data storage; however, they can also be used as dedicated servers for many types of databases, Web pages, or system backup.

Video Area Networks

Rather than find a way to work FireWire's benefits into existing network protocols harmoniously, some manufacturers have dedicated themselves to developing a new network architecture tailored to the demands of multichannel broadcast operations. The term for this emerging category is *video area network*.

Designed to meet the networking and storage needs of companies that produce and distribute audio and video content, video area networks are based primarily on FireWire efficiencies.

A pioneering company in this effort is Omneon, which developed a Networked Content Server System composed of network interfaces, packet switches, disc-based storage subsystems, and system software. The Omneon system consists of modular components attached to each other via FireWire cables that manage data storage, video transport within the network, and the connection of external devices to the network.

The architecture is basically a specialized SAN configured as a NAS that scales to 16 terabytes within a single distributed

The Omneon Networked Content Server is a FireWire-based solution for collaborative environments. Any video production can be streamlined by centralizing footage storage on an array of MPS Switches that route files to each remote workstation and use dedicated MediaPorts for centralized input and output, giving every networked computer the ability to simultaneously share video streams collected on a single storage system.

file system designed to accommodate the wide range of data types required in video editing applications. Because it's FireWire based, the Omneon network handles isochronous audio/video channels and asynchronous data simultaneously, and can scale to 3.2 gigabits per second on optical fiber. Already installed in many professional studios, the Omneon network demonstrates how FireWire can retain high-band-width streams at fixed latency.

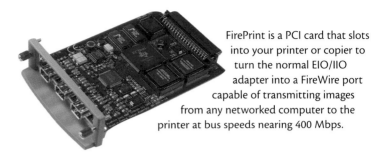

FirePrint is a PCI card that slots into your printer or copier to turn the normal EIO/IIO adapter into a FireWire port capable of transmitting images from any networked computer to the printer at bus speeds nearing 400 Mbps.

PRINTING OVER FIREWIRE NETWORKS

For some time, users of high-speed printers and copiers have hoped that FireWire technology could be universally adapted to their hardware. Although a few products have already been announced, IEEE 1394b, FireWire's next-generation specification, aims to tackle the complex world of printers.

One product that provides a quick solution is FirePrint, a PCI card that slots into your printer or copier to turn the EIO/IIO adapter into a FireWire port capable of bus speeds nearing 400 Mbps. Any computer on the FireWire network will see this printer as a shared local printer, though not necessarily as a network printer.

Unlike other suggested implementations of a FireWire printing bus, FirePrint has no special software requirements for the target printer: If a computer can see it on the local network, there's no added storage buffer or time spent transmitting the printed image to the device.

As important as it is today, FireWire promises to play an even greater role in future digital filmmaking by providing an easy means of connecting a vast array of consumer electronics (stereo equipment, televisions, and computers) to create a fast and easy-to-configure multimedia home network. With the advent of the IEEE 1394b standard, several networking issues will be addressed. These advances, combined with developments in intelligent switching and mass storage technology, bode well for FireWire's future as a video networking technology.

MK12

The five computer animators who comprise the Kansas City studio MK12 are all well-rounded artists who work closely to produce highly experimental videos. However, lately, the animators have decided to tackle projects that put some distance between team members. To meet the demands of clients as far ranging as the Sci-Fi Channel and Nickelodeon, the chain-smoking members of MK12—Ben Radatz, Tim Fisher, Matt Fraction, Jed Carter, and Shaun Hamontree—have learned to split up and spread out in their Midwest shop by collaborating over a FireWire network.

The firm connected its eight workstations using midprice AV equipment and FireWire storage drives running over a Mac OSX server using FireNet software. Although this configuration didn't involve a massive investment on the part of the studio, it has provided the artists with a unique advantage when competing for big-budget television projects under extremely tight deadlines. It's a working method that allows MK12 to sprinkle its demo reel with a mix of 3D animation, photo-realistic artwork, motion graphics, and slick video effects.

For its latest experimental film, MK12 used a centralized FireWire storage device to store hundreds of high-resolution project files over a network consisting of FireWire cables, FireNet software, and a Mac OSX operating system running on a PowerMac G4. Here, artist Ben Radatz accesses a still photo to create ray-tracings in Maya software for 3D effects in the finished film.

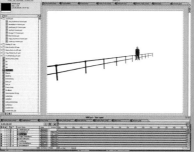

While Radatz works on his portion of the project, artist Matt Faction grabs the same frame of footage from a storage partition on the FireWire network and applies motion graphics from vector artwork in Adobe After Effects. He works on a proxy file to make numerous revisions before adapting his final changes to the source footage.

While Radatz and Faction work right up to the final deadline in their 3D and animation programs, artist Jed Carter is busy applying filter effects to images in Photoshop and After Effects, referencing the footage that resides on the storage server. When all elements have been approved, Carter combines them into a single composition in After Effects and adds motion blur before preparing the project for final export.

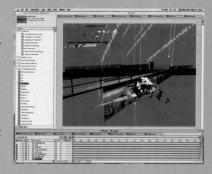

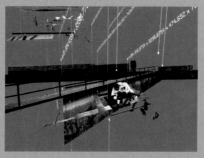

The finished composition is now ready for output to a number of formats, including DVD and BetaSP for delivery to clients, broadcasters, and film festivals. Tim Fisher, the administrator of the MK12 FireWire network, can now archive the project knowing that all related files are stored in a single place. The completed short, *Infinity*, appears on the FireWire Filmmaking DVD included with this book.

chapter eight

finishing your movies

One of the most difficult parts of moviemaking is completing a project. Editing and special effects seem to take forever to finish, and they're lonely, subjective jobs. And once you've completed those tasks, you still have decisions to make about output formats, saving your final DV movie, and archiving sound elements, title artwork, and project files. The last of these decisions—how to archive your project elements over the long term—is especially important because DV footage takes up a lot of hard disk space. In other words, you won't want to store finished films on your computer for too long.

Distribution and archiving are extremely important issues for digital creators.

If you plan to premiere your movie on TV for friends and family, you can easily create copies of the video on tape formats like miniDV and VHS. But once you're ready to pass your movie along to others, several FireWire devices can speed backup and help record to tape, CD-ROM, DVD, and DAT drives. You can also save projects with separate audio tracks, multiformatted content, and Web compression settings for streaming video online.

The last step for aspiring moviemakers is distributing their DV films on popular formats like DVD. Today, there are widely available tools (for both Macs and PCs) for developing personal MPEG-encoded DVDs. This chapter outlines the production steps entailed in preparing your footage for these applications. It also details the steps filmmakers must take to prepare their final movies for submission to a tape-to-film transfer facility, which will blow up their images to 35mm prints.

Exporting and Archiving Movies

It's neither safe nor practical to store DV footage on your computer hard disk for long periods of time—and even if it were, you'd likely need that disk space for your next project. Thus, you need to explore your options for exporting final versions of your movie and archiving essential elements so that you can reconstruct the project in the event of loss or damage.

If you're exporting your movie to a compressed file format for CD-ROM or Web distribution, you'll want to save a full-resolution version of the project before you begin compressing footage. This way, you'll have a master file to refer back to if a system error or power interruption causes you to lose or corrupt your finished project.

Exporting to DV Tapes

Obviously, the easiest and most economical way to export your finished movie is back to a DV tape in your FireWire camcorder. Almost all of today's DV editing applications export footage over FireWire to a camcorder or deck. Simply select the Export command from the File menu when you're ready to transfer footage to tape. If a FireWire recording device is not properly connected, the application will issue a warning indicating that the power is not turned on or the tape

In most DV applications, you can select the Export command from the File menu when you're ready to transfer your footage to tape.

is not loaded. In most cases, you'll have to wait a moment before your DV device is ready, allowing time for the camera's tape heads to rewind and position themselves for recording. In most camcorders, this only takes a few seconds.

You also have the option of providing a "leader" to your exported footage, several seconds of blackness to prepare the viewer for the coming movie. When copying your footage to a VHS tape or another VCR, this black leader eases the

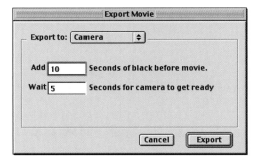

When exporting to tape, especially when giving footage to a broadcast studio, you should create at least seven seconds of blank leader (or black-striped tape) before and after your movie. It's particularly important to have a proper amount of space between multiple clips placed on the same tape.

transition from your television's white noise to the beginning of the movie.

For archiving footage, nothing can match the DV format for speed, capacity, and affordability. DV tapes are durable, compact, and inexpensive, making them ideal for archiving your FireWire footage. They also provide the best means of transferring footage to different media without losing quality or resolution.

However, these tapes aren't impervious to deterioration or damage, so keep them in a protective case and avoid exposing them to extreme changes in temperature. You can further protect your archived footage by switching the small tab on the videotape cartridge into the protected position—a good idea since it can prevent others from accidentally erasing the tape or recording over your footage.

Check the instructions that come with your tapes for additional tips on long-term care. If you intend to archive footage on DV videotapes for long stretches of time, make sure you take your tapes out of storage semi-annually and fast-forward and rewind them to ensure that they remain in proper working condition.

If your project is extremely important (say it has tremendous historical value or documents vital evidence), you may wish to store your tapes at an off-site repository. Many security services now offer climate-controlled safe houses for long-term archival of important digital data.

Copying to VHS Tape

Once you've transferred your movie to a digital videotape, you can use the audio/video cables supplied with your DV camcorder to watch your movie on a standard television set.

You can also use these cables to connect the camcorder to your VCR and copy your movie to a VHS tape for distribution.

Remember, though: DV footage output to VHS tapes suffers significantly in quality because the digital data is turned into analog signals inside the VCR. This means that VHS tapes are not a suitable format for archival footage, and you should never consider analog tape a permanent solution for storing your final footage. For complete guidelines on copying from DV tapes to VHS, consult the manufacturer's instructions included with your camcorder and VCR.

Movies for Web or Wireless Devices

Many editing programs now feature export options that instantly compress video for streaming over the Internet. As mentioned earlier, however, these compressed formats seriously degrade the pixel information and resolution of your digital movie. Although these formats are fine for online viewing, they're not adequate for saving your final movie. Make sure you have successfully exported your projects to lossless formats on storage media or DV tape before selecting files for compression.

Using Preset Compression

That said, most applications' export options for Web compression do an excellent job of turning your DV footage into compact files for distribution over dial-up modem or high-speed Internet connections. Web site designers can easily incorporate these compressed movies into their Web pages or offer them for download on a Web server. This powerful exchange of desktop video over the Internet makes every computer owner his or her own network—able to offer unique programming to the entire world. By using the Internet, moviemakers

can share their work instantly—instead of being rejected by film festivals and studio executives.

Applications tailored to Web moviemaking usually include powerful compression software to streamline the export of finished footage to the Internet. In most cases, predefined compression settings produce excellent Web-ready files— often making them compact enough to attach as video clips to email messages. You will rarely need to change these compression settings because they're fine-tuned to produce exceptional playback across a variety of systems and speeds.

There will be times, however, when more experienced users will wish to tinker with the advanced compression settings to get better clarity or faster movement from their video streams. For example, web movies that feature text may need to be adjusted for clarity, while action sequences in other scenes are fine-tuned for smoother motion. You should alter the preset functions of compression software only if you have a good understanding of video compression and want to customize the settings for specific project requirements. Even then, advanced users will probably produce better results by using the presets as a baseline, and then subtly adjusting the settings to meet their needs.

> **TIP**
>
> *COMPRESSION UTILITIES*
> *CLEANER 5 IS A MUST-HAVE UTIL-ITY FOR BATCH PROCESSING STREAMING VIDEO CLIPS, SETTING THE QUALITY OF THE COMPRESSED MOVIES IN QUICKTIME, REAL, AVI, AND MPEG-1 AND WINDOWS MEDIA PLAYER FORMATS.*

Preparing Video for Streaming

The image quality of streaming movies differs dramatically from that of downloadable QuickTime files: Because footage for streaming movies is compressed without as much detail, you can't guarantee that your pictures will look good to the viewer. You can, however, guarantee that it will arrive in timely fashion. And because video streams are buffered in three-second chunks in a small cache file rather than saved on your hard drive, you can save or replay them offline.

What started as an audio plug-in for browsers has grown into a multi-faceted multimedia solution. Real Player streams compressed movies over the Internet and presents them in your Web browser for immediate playback. Although Real Player doesn't support a wide variety of formats, it does cover popular ones like MP3, JPEG, MPEG, and Flash.

With streaming video, the soundtrack is usually delivered audibly and without interruption. Whether you choose downloads or streaming for your movies, pay close attention to the audio quality of your movies and recompress them using different settings if the results are not acceptable. If you're interested in streaming video from your own desktop or home-made server, Apple's QuickTime as well as several other solutions provide easy ways to send clips over a local network or the Web. (See the "Web References" appendix in the back of the book for a list of manufacturers' Web sites.)

FROM FIREWIRE TO FILM

The promise of video-to-film transfer has recently attracted the attention of major studios (including Dreamworks SKG, Universal, and Twentieth Century Fox), and several digital independent features have already had their theatrical releases on traditional film stock. Indeed, several of the 2001 Sundance Film Festival feature films (*Women in Film, Tape,* and *Things*

Behind the Sun) originated on videotape—news that shook the Indie Film world.

Don't feel you have to transfer your video project to film to submit or showcase your work at a film festival, however: Nearly every major film festival has now adopted some sort of digital projection system to display video projects. But many directors still prefer the aesthetic of film. So they prepare their digital footage by converting video formats to the 24-fps rate used in film to produce a more desirable effect before transferring their movie to film stock or preparing it for digital projection.

When viewing video footage transferred to 35mm film, these conversion techniques achieve results ranging from barely credible to visually indistinguishable. The process of converting interlaced fields into complete frames is a vital part of transferring video to film, but some methods simply average the fields, then throw away or blend frames to arrive at final frame-rate conversion. In addition, many transfer facilities use their own proprietary methods, which can create mixed results.

If you intend to create a film transfer of your video project for theatrical release, make sure you consult with a film transfer house well in advance. In some cases, it's wise to test different scenes on specific film stock before you begin shooting your movie. A resource list of video-to-film transfer facilities appears in the Appendix II at the end of this book.

Preparing Footage for Film Transfer

As traditional cinematographers and directors know, film labs are anything but fast and affordable. Most charge an hourly rate, which means that any indecision on your part can translate to a huge bill. If you wish to avoid the expense and backlog of a transfer facility, you can prepare your own footage for film by using Magic Bullet software.

With a large, custom-created set of filters for Adobe After Effects, Magic Bullet alters pixels by their YUV values—it doesn't average, throw away, or blend frames to get a simple

This scene was shot with an NTSC miniDV camcorder under existing lighting conditions. The brightness of the 30-fps footage and the crispness of the camera motion give away the fact that it was shot on video.

Once the Magic Bullet process is performed, through a series of filter settings in Adobe After Effects, the scene is reduced to 24 fps and appears with a "film look," after adjustments to the pixels' YUV values and motion blur have been made.

conversion. Instead, Magic Bullet allows you to control the "look" of video frames, then selectively discards video fields to re-create image data from those deleted pixels. In most cases, the software must interpolate data generated using pattern-recognition algorithms. To derive a proper frame-rate conversion, Magic Bullet reconforms the linear contrast curves of video formats to emulate the characteristics of film. The extraction tools in the Magic Bullet package allow you to control the video artifact and precise film grain properties.

Ideally, you should apply the Magic Bullet process just described at the beginning of your production cycle, just after clips have been captured into the computer. This way, each clip can be color corrected individually, and the footage becomes locked as a 24-fps digital file that can be visually altered in almost any way imaginable. When your project is ready for output to film, the finalized 24-fps "digital answer print" is sent to a film transfer facility where each frame is seamlessly transferred to celluloid film. Magic Bullet footage even takes on the properties of film when recompressed to television formats or as downloadable video for the Web.

To get the most out of Magic Bullet, you should begin with footage that's uncompressed 10-bit color data (though it also works at the 8-bit color depths common among desktop programs). High-resolution source footage ultimately renders finer results to film; filmmakers on the lower end of the DV range should choose a miniDV camcorder that offers good imaging, the most lines of resolution, and a 25-fps frame rate (PAL format).

Most filmmakers who plan to transfer their video to film begin with a PAL-version camcorder rather than an NTSC one, because it's easier to convert PAL's 25fps frame rate to film's 24 fps. Recommended cameras include the Sony PD150 PAL (which captures 625 lines of resolution at 25 fps), the Sony DSR-500WS PAL miniDV camcorder (whose native16-by-9 chipset processes video at 10-bit color depth), and the Sony DVW-790WS PAL DigiBeta 16-by-9 camera with 10-bit, 4:2:2 processing. At the top end of HD video production is the Sony HDW-F900, a true progressive-frame 24Pcamera that captures images at 1,920-by-1,080-pixel resolution (George Lucas' choice for digital shooting on the *Star Wars* sequels).

Distributing Movies on CDs or DVDs

In addition to tape or film transfers, you can also output your movies to a lossless QuickTime file format and store them as digital data on a number of media types: digital-audio tapes (DATs), magneto-optical removable cartridges, or CDs and DVDs. Popular disc formats provide you with not only a means of archiving your finished footage in pristine quality, but also a way to easily create versions of your movies for dissemination to prospective buyers or clients—a huge advantage over traditional film projects. Today, most homes and businesses have CD or DVD players—which means your movie can be viewed at full quality.

Saving Your Movie for CD-ROM

When you export a QuickTime file from your editing application, you'll have a variety of compression options. For archival purposes, it's important to select a format that's "lossless"—that is, one that doesn't recompress the DV codec into another format. If you have chosen a QuickTime compression format for email or small Web movies—any file that presents your movie in a size or aspect ratio that differs from the original—an algorithm will reduce the large DV file into a compact minimovie. And in so doing, degrade the quality of your picture. Make sure your QuickTime files are saved in an ideal format for playback on CD-ROM.

You don't need an AC adapter or battery pack to burn CDs with the Bus-Powered VST Portable CD-R/W from SmartDisk. It's really three CD burners in one, writing CD-ROM, CD-R, and CD-R/W media.

DIGITAL BUSINESS CARDS

Let's talk business. You're a creative video professional working on stunning effects for the film and television industries. When prospective clients ask you to explain the power and excitement of adding full-motion images to their communications—in short, what you do for a living—you hand them your business card. Except that it's really your portfolio, burned onto a CD-ROM!

Today, a number of national vendors produce these elegant digital business cards by duplicating CDs and trimming them into custom-shaped calling cards. You simply prepare your movies in compressed formats of up to 40MB (so that you can show your flashiest work as self-running demos, Flash presentations, QuickTime movies, or audio samples) and send off a master disc for duplication. Once the CD-ROM has been created, cut, trimmed to standard biz card size, and slipped into a custom sleeve, you can begin your marketing campaign in digital style. Most of these odd-size discs come with a special molded design (or raised bumps) that help them fit snuggly into a computer drive cradle. You can even imprint your logo or artwork on the face of the CD card. It makes an ideal electronic media kit or demo reel, and a short run of 500 printed and pressed CDs can cost as little as $2 each to distribute.

If you've already backed up to tape a master version of your project and simply wish to compress a promotional version for inclusion on a CD-ROM (with 650MB capacity), you'll need to use a QuickTime compression format to shrink your large DV files to fit onto a single disc. Because of their relatively small capacity, CD-ROMs are not ideal for archiving raw video footage; however, they do provide a great way to distribute electronic press kits that include movie clips and other promotional material.

CDs are also great for archiving audio tracks separately, keeping them on a different media type than the master tape recordings. CDs can also record sound elements as playable audio tracks, which you can then listen to in a car stereo or home entertainment system when you need to find a specific audio clip.

There are hundreds of fast, inexpensive FireWire CD drives available today that can read or write (*burn*) your files directly to affordable CDs. However, if your wish is to mass-produce a number of CDs, it's better to find a local duplication service or check the Internet for vendors that offer economies of scale. Several vendors will even create promotional CDs that are custom cut in interesting shapes—even down to the size of a business card—so that you can distribute your movies in a handy, digital form.

DAT Recorders

Many video professionals still prefer the reliability and cost of DAT for backup over magneto-optical media, CDs, or DVDs. In most cases, DAT drives employ a read-after-write technology, which provides higher data integrity than other types of drives. What's more, the medium is more forgiving than videotape when it comes to years of neglect. Designed for use with compressed audio/video and multimedia data, today's FireWire DAT drives have been optimized to provide the increased storage that video professionals require. Each inexpensive DAT can now hold as much as 6GB of data—ideal for massive files, video with irregular frame sizes, or clips of long takes that cannot be archived on DV tape or other media.

Do-It-Yourself DVD Solutions

As writable DVD drives and media have become more accessible and cost-effective, many desktop moviemakers have started distributing their movies on DVDs. As one of the simplest ways to share movies, DVDs offer video creators unprecedented project control, from creation to distribution—without sacrificing quality. DVDs come in two formats: discs that save computer data, and discs that play movies on TVs. In some cases, movies and computer data reside on the same disc.

For archival purposes, DVDs offer as much as 4.7GB of data storage on a single side. Because most commercial DVDs are single-sided, their storage space is limited. However, several manufacturers are now making cartridge systems that write to both sides of a DVD, providing more than 9GB per cartridge.

For viewing, DVD discs need to be formatted to carry MPEG-compressed footage. That means you must use special authoring software to compress your DV footage before you can burn it onto a DVD and play it on a TV. Fortunately, MPEG-2 compression for DVD is incredibly close to the resolution of a full DV stream, so you won't notice a change in the quality of your movie.

Several consumer-level DV editing solutions now ship with simple authoring tools for nonexperts. Apple's iDVD, for example, is entry-level software for assembling video clips for DVD discs and recording them directly from a Macintosh computer

For inexpensive removable media, look no further than the FireWire RAV6 DAT drive from Indigita. Available as an internal drive or external enclosure, it uses an advanced Digital Video Data Storage (DVDS) format to store 6GB of native DV data on a standard DDS-2 tape, which typically costs $10.

As its name implies, Pioneer has long been a frontrunner in DVD drives that write and read DVD-RW, DVD-R, CD-R, and CD-RW media, as well as read CD-ROM and DVD-ROM discs. These drives offer as much as 4.7GB of storage on a single-sided DVD and full authoring capability.

With the ability to write more than two hours of video on a 4.7GB DVD-R disc, the QPS Fire DVDBurner is perfect for authoring and archiving. It also writes to industry-standard DVD-RAM discs for backup or scratch disks so you can experiment and save different versions of your favorite projects.

equipped with an internal DVD burner (sometimes called a SuperDrive). Many of these simpler tools don't allow you to create custom interfaces or interactive controls; you use them solely to transfer video streams into MPEG-2 video for burning to DVD discs. Full-featured DVD authoring applications, in contrast, give you greater control over the look and functionality of your DVD movies. In addition to providing professional MPEG encoding, these programs let you add moving menus, Web links, and interactive controls like multiangle viewing to your movies.

If your computer does not include an internal DVD-R drive, you can purchase a third-party DVD burner from manufacturers like Pioneer Electronics, Philips, and QPS. Most models have FireWire interfaces to accelerate the transfer of footage to DVD. These devices record data or MPEG-2 footage to the DVD-R disc as a write-once format (like the CD-R is to audio) compatible with home DVD players. Once the disc has been burned, you can't reuse it or place additional movies on it.

With both CD and DVD disc burners at their disposal, filmmakers can easily find clamshell covers and jewel boxes to distribute their discs in a professional manner. You can also

TIP

Video CDs

SOME MOVIEMAKERS TRY TO CIRCUMVENT THE HIGHER-PRICED DVD BURNERS OR DVD-R BLANK MEDIA BY BURNING THEIR CAPTURED CLIPS DIRECTLY TO RECORDABLE CDs—TO A FORMAT CALLED THE VIDEO CD. VIDEO CDs ARE HIGHLY COMPRESSED MPEG 1 VIDEO/AUDIO CLIPS THAT WORK IN SOME DVD PLAYERS BUT OFTEN DISPLAY AT RESOLUTION WELL BELOW BROADCAST TELEVISION.

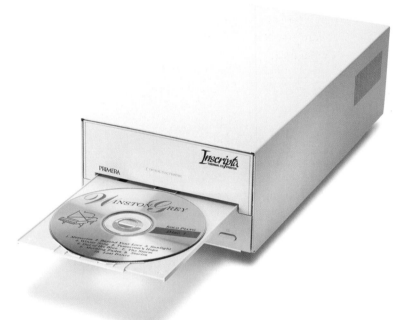

One way to make your digital promo reel look professional is to finish the CD or DVD face with thermal-printed artwork. Using the Inscripta CD printer from Primera Technology, you get 610-by-305-dpi resolution, highly scratch- and smudge-resistant and waterproof inks, and a slick shine.

use any number of prepackaged kits to customize and print color sleeves for these cases. Although some CD-labels run through ink-jet printers and adhere to the face of the disc itself, other thermal CD printers will even allow you to print designs directly onto the medium for a screen-printed look.

The Orphanage

The Orphanage is one of the pioneering companies in digital post-production. Its founders, Jonathan Rothbart, Scott Stewart, and Stuart Maschwitz, left their posts as special-effects artists at Industrial Light and Magic in 1999 to dedicate themselves to independent film and video projects that would stretch the limits of what could be done with desktop computers and off-the-shelf software.

Quickly establishing a reputation for creating world-class visual effects for independent directors, these talented men (who previously toiled on Hollywood blockbusters like *Star Trek: First Contact*, *Twister*, and *The Lost World: Jurassic Park 2*) were now offering ways to do things "cheaper, faster, and better" than other digital studios.

The company recently co-produced the short film *bigLove*, shot with the new Sony HDW-F900 24-frame, progressive-scan HD camera. The short was finished by the Orphans in their San Francisco facility, transferred to 35mm stock by the firm Swiss Effects, and eventually projected to wild acclaim at the Sundance Film Festival.

SHOOTING 24P FOOTAGE FOR TRANSFER TO FILM

Orphanage principals were present on the set of *bigLove* to provide consultation for shooting that would alter the outcome of visual effects, titles, and final film output. Here, Stu Maschwitz confers with cinematographer Patricia Van Over aside the Sony 24P camcorder, equipped with Panavision lenses. It was extremely important to advise the camera crew on how shots might complicate special effects in post-production.

Cofounders Scott Stewart and Jonathan Rothbart check the 24P footage on a widescreen reference monitor. The entire film was captured in a 16:9 letterboxed format for the most cinematic look in projection.

After checking the script and storyboards, actress Mary McCormack is rigged to special wires that will suspend her in a scene that reveals her unusual strength. Unlike translucent fishing line used in many smaller effects, these industrial wires are white so that computer artists can clearly identify them.

After the 24P footage is captured as uncompressed 10-bit video data, the wire removal process begins. Using low-resolution proxy footage, artists used a "clean plate" reference image of the kitchen to fill in areas where the wires appear.

The final shot looks seamless, as if the actress were suspended by nothing more than the strength of her own arm. At this point, the scene is color corrected and integrated with other clips in editing.

As one of the first test sites for Apple's DVD Studio Pro, the Orphanage created interactive menus that let prospective clients see examples of their work and watch the development of digital projects as they are transferred to film.

appendixes and index

Appendix A:

Web References

The following list contains the Web sites of products and companies listed in this book, as well as some informative and entertaining destinations for aspiring moviemakers. For a single resource page with all of these hyperlinks, bookmark the FireWire Filmmaking site at www.peachpit.com/books/firewire.

FireWire Discussions and News Groups

1394 Trade Association
www.1394ta.org

Cineweb's Connections
www.cineweb.com

Desktop Video
desktopvideo.miningco.com

Desktop Video Newsgroup
rec.video.desktop

DV Central
www.dvcentral.org

Global DVC Group
www.global-dvc.org

Mac Digital Video Resources
www.postforum.pair.com

Movie Production Newsgroup
rec.arts.movies.production

Multimedia Tools
www.multimediatools.com

Video Production Newsgroup
rec.video.production

FireWire Cameras and Accessories

Bogen
www.bogenphoto.com

Canon USA
www.canondv.com

Foveon
www.foveon.com

Hardigg's Cases
www.hardigg.com

JVC Electronics
www.jvc-america.com

Markertek Video Supply
www.markertek.com

Nikon USA
www.nikonusa.com

NRG Research
www.nrgresearch.com

Panasonic
www.panasonic.com

Sony Electronics
www.sel.sony.com

Sharp
www.sharpusa.com

Video Smith
www.videosmith.com

Moviemaking Magazines and Resources

DV Magazine
www.dv.com

DV Format
www.dvformat.com

DVEreview - Newsletter
www.dvereview.com

Filmmaker Magazine
www.filmmag.com

The Internet Movie Database
www.imdb.com

The Movie Sound FAQ
www.moviesoundpage.com

Pro Audio Network
www.digitalprosound.com

Production Hub
www.productionhub.com

RES **magazine**
www.resmag.com

Sightsound.com
www.sightsound.com

Videography **magazine**
www.videography.com

Videomaker Magazine
www.videomaker.com

Software Vendors

After Effects, Premiere
www.adobe.com

ColorTheory
www.toolfarm.com

EchoFire
www.syntheticaperture.com

Final Cut Pro, iMovie
www.apple.com

FrameThief
www.framethief.com

Microsoft Media Player
www.microsoft.com/windows/mediaplayer

Magic Bullet
www.theorphanage.com

Maya
www.aliaswavefront.com

Media100, EditDV, Cleaner 5
www.media100.com

Peak DV
www.bias-inc.com

Real Networks
www.realnetworks.com

Studio 7
www.pinnaclesys.com

Vegas Video
www.sonicfoundry.com

Xpress
www.avid.com

FireWire Hardware Manufacturers

1394 FireStation
www.1394firestation.com

AITech
www.aitech.com

Canto
www.canto.com

Digital Voodoo
www.digitalvoodoo.com

Dynamic Network Factory
www.dynamicnetworkfactory.com

Gear Preview
www.gearpreview.com

Imagine
www.imagineproducts.com

Indigita
www.indigita.com

Epson Printers
www.epson.com

Fantom Drives
www.fantomdrives.com

FirePower
www.firepower .com

FireWire Watch
www.fw-watch.com

Focus Enhancements
www.focusenhancements.com

LaCie
www.lacie.com

MicroNet
www.micronet .com

Medea
www.medeacorp.com

Omneon
www.omneon.com

Pioneer Electronics
www.pioneerelectronics.com

Powerfile
www.dvdjukebox.com

Primera Technology
www.primeratech.com

QPS
www.qps-inc.com

Ratoc
www.ratoctech.com

SmartDisk
www.smartdisk.com

SoftAcoustik
www.softacoustik.com

Videonics
www.videonics.com

VST Technology
www.vsttech.com

Umax
www.umax.com

Unibrain
www.unibrain.com

Profiled FireWire Filmmakers

Bryan Boyce
www.dangeroussquid.com

Damaged Californians
www.damagedcalifornians.com

Rolf Gibbs
www.rolfgibbs.com

MK12
www.mk12.com

The Orphanage
www.theorphanage.com

APPENDIX B:

USING THE DVD

The accompanying DVD provides a showcase of exemplary films made with FireWire technology. To view these movies, simply place the disc into your DVD player and navigate the interactive menus. The disc also includes a number of free trial versions of commercial or shareware software designed for FireWire filmmaking efforts. These are provided as install files, accessible from any computer capable of reading DVD-ROM media. If the software isn't compatible with your system, don't lose heart: These manufacturers are working diligently to provide solutions across all platforms, and new vendors are springing up daily. Keep your eyes on the Web for other applications and updates that can help you reap the remarkable benefits of FireWire in your desktop video productions.

The following software is featured on the DVD-ROM portion of the disc:

DVLog Pro (Chapter 4)

Version: 1.0

System requirements: Built-in FireWire port (or free PCI or PC Bus slot); Windows 2000, Me, or 98SE with DirectX-8 installed; Pentium 266-MHz 800x600 resolution monitor; 64MB RAM; 100MB free disk space.

DVLog Pro software automates your logging and capturing sessions. This unlimited trial version lets you use the logging interface, scene detection, and search functions, but file saving functions and printing are disabled. DVLog Pro uses the Microsoft DV standard drivers supplied with Windows 2000, Me, and 98SE. This disc also includes DV Detector for Windows, which tests your system to be sure only Microsoft's DV drivers are installed and working properly. Download this utility if the demo does not function properly (no video), or if you simply want to test your computer. DVLog Pro is not compatible with Windows NT. For additional information on DVLog Pro, visit www.imagineproducts.com.

Echo Fire (Chapter 5)

Version: 2.0.3

System requirements: Power-PC-based Mac with OS 8.6 or later, QuickTime 4.1.2 or later, and a FireWire port.

EchoFire streams DV footage to an NTSC or PAL video monitor instead of your computer monitor for accurate previews of your designs in Adobe After Effects and Photoshop. It works with any Macintosh and any video output device with a QuickTime Video Output Component, including Apple's built-in FireWire ports, Digital Voodoo D1 Desktop, and Pinnacle Systems CineWave and Targa 1000/2000, as well as Aurora Igniter and Fuse, and Media 100 display cards. FireWire users will need a camcorder, VTR, or similar device to convert FireWire to video.

This fully functional demonstration version of the software can be installed and used for 72 hours without a serial number. Also included is a 60-page manual in Adobe Acrobat (PDF) format. To obtain a serial number, visit the Synthetic Aperture site at www.syntheticaperture.com.

ColorTheoryDV (Chapter 5)

Version: 1.2

System requirements: Power PC-based Macintosh running OS 8.6 or later, QuickTime 4.1.2 or later, and a FireWire port.

ColorTheory is a digital color wheel that designers can use to quickly analyze hundreds of color schemes and find harmonious red, yellow, and blue (RYB) combinations for logos and artwork. ColorTheory also allows broadcast designers to preview these color choices directly on their NTSC/PAL monitors. As a stand-alone application, ColorTheory DV works with Apple's new operating system OSX, as well as Adobe Photoshop and After Effects plug-ins that are supported in Apple's Final Cut Pro, Pinnacle Systems' Commotion, Discreet Combustion, and Avid Media Composer (when used with the

Profound Effects' Elastic Gasket).This trial version also features five free Adobe After Effects plug-ins (you keep them whether or not you buy ColorTheory): CT ColorSwatch, CT Location, CT Dial, CT Slider, and CT Checkbox. ColorTheory DV has a list price of $249. Both products are now shipping for the Macintosh. Visit www.toolfarm.com for more information.

Frame Thief (Chapter 6)

Version: 2.0

System requirements: Mac OS 8.6, 9, or X, or a Power PC-based Mac (G3 or better recommended) with at least 128 MB of RAM and 200 MB of hard drive space, QuickTime 4.1.2 or later, CarbonLib 1.2.5, and a QuickTime-compatible video source (DV, QuickCam, etc.).

FrameThief, a stop-motion animation toolset for the Mac, acts as a video frame grabber and is compatible with nearly all Mac video capture devices—from Webcams to DV camcorders. FrameThief is a shareware application; the fee for personal use is $40 (which goes to support the development efforts of the application and to provide quality technical support). For more information, visit www.framethief.com.

FireNet (Chapter 7)

Version: 2.0

System requirements: Mac OS 9 or above, FireWire Support and Enabler files must be 2.5 or above

FireNet is Ethernet emulation software that works seamlessly with all existing Ethernet-compatible software and hardware. FireNet supports all of the standard Ethernet protocols, including IPX/SPX, NetBEUI, TCP/IP, and AppleTalk. FireNet supports both Windows and Macintosh operating systems as well as mixed (PC and Mac) networks. This fully functional version will run for 30 minutes between reboots so that you can evaluate it fully. To use all FireNet features with no time limit, you need an authorization key number. There are versions of FireNet available for Windows 98SE/Me/2000 workstations and Windows 2000 servers. Visit www.unibrain.com for more information.

Using the Trial Software

To install the project files for use with the tutorial lessons:

1   Insert the FireWire Filmmaking DVD disc (provided in this book's back cover) into a DVD-ROM-capable disk drive on your computer.

2   Locate the Trial Software folder and select the software for your platform.

3   Double-click the installer icons to run the software.

INDEX

broadcast television, 69, 79–82

broadcast video, 79–82

broadcasts, live, 67–72

burning CDs, 119, 120, 121

burning DVDs, 121

Burns, Ken, 96

business cards, digital, 119

C

cables, 47–48, 83

camcorders. *See* video cameras

cameras. *See* analog video cameras; digital
    cameras; digital video cameras

candlelight, 32

Canon USA Web site, 127

Canon XL-1 camera, 11, 12

Canto Cumulus software, 66

Canto Web site, 129

capture cards, 46–47, 68

capturing video, 55–72

    batch capturing, 64

    converting analog video to DV video, 55

    described, 55

    direct capture, 67–70

    to disk, 67–70

    to DVD, 70

    live from camera, 70–72

    with timecode, 63–64

    to the Web, 71–72

CardBus adapters, 47

Carter, Jed, 112

catalog software, 66–67

CCD images, 15

CCDs (charge-coupled devices), 9

CD burners, 119, 120, 121

CD drives, 120

CD jukebox, 106

CD-R burners, 106

CDs

    burning, 119, 120, 121

    labels for, 121

    movies on, 119–120

    sleeves for, 121

    storing audio tracks on, 119

    video, 121

charge-coupled devices. *See* CCDs

chromakey effects, 34, 37

chromakey scenes, 35–36

chromatic aberration, 24

chromatic color, 34

chrominance problems, 69

Cinemotion, 38

Cineweb's Connections Web site, 127

clips

    deleting, 62

    described, 55

    destination of, 58

    exporting as image sequences, 92–93

    importing, 55–56

    marking for import, 57–58

    maximum length, 58–59

    naming, 65–66

    previewing, 75–76

    setting markers for, 57

    size of, 57, 58–59

    space required for, 58

    storing, 62

    timecode captures, 63

    transferring to computer, 55–56

    viewing, 58

close-up shots, 33

CMYK format, 81

Coffey, Scott, 17

color

    24-bit, 83

    capturing, 6

    chromatic, 34

    costumes, 31–33

    digital video and, 29

    light and, 30

    one-chip cameras and, 10

    polarizing filters and, 22

    RGB, 5

    saturation, 34, 81

    three-chip cameras and, 10

colorizing video, 21

ColorTheory DV software, 81, 128, 131–132

component video, 86

composite AV adapter cable, 83

composite video, 83

compression, 6–7

    4:1:1 compression, 34

    camera movement and, 38

    dark settings and, 33

    described, 6

    MPEG-2, 120, 121

    patterns and, 33

    preset, 116

    QuickTime, 119

    Web movies and, 116

    zooming and, 33

computers

    adding capture card to, 46–47

    connecting camera to, 45

    connecting multiple computers, 105–106

    connecting two computers, 104–105

    laptop, 47, 79, 82

    transferring DV clips to, 55–56

contrast, 22, 29, 34

conversion lenses, 23–24

converters, 23–24, 34, 49–50, 68

copiers, 111

copyright detection software, 49

costumes, 31–33

cross-platform issues, 46, 105–106

Cumulus software, 66

D

D1 Desktop 128HD card, 86
Damaged Californians, 70
DAT drives, 120
DAT recorders, 28, 120
DATs (digital-audio tapes), 119
daylight, 36
degaussing switch, 81
deleting clips, 62
Desktop Video newsgroup, 127
Desktop Video Web site, 127
device control, 56–57
devices
    AC power and, 47
    analog, 82
    battery power and, 47
    daisy chain, 48, 56
    drivers for, 47
    file-sharing, 106
    hot-pluggable, 4, 56, 103
    large storage volumes, 59–60
    monitors. *See* monitors
    options for, 79–84
    printers, 97–98
    RAID systems, 60–61
    scan converters, 82–83
    scanners, 97–98
    sharing, 104
    storage. *See* storage devices
diffusers, 30–31
diffusion filters, 22
DigiBeta (Digital Betacam) format, 12
digital audio, 8
digital-audio tapes (DATs), 119
Digital Betacam (DigiBeta) format, 12
digital business cards, 119
digital camcorders. *See* digital video
    cameras

digital cameras. *See also* digital video
    cameras
    advantages, 4
    audio and, 8
    capturing still images, 95
    choosing, 1–17
    color and, 6
    described, 3–4
    FireWire-equipped, 94–95
    playheads, 5
    resolution, 96
    shooting tips, 19–41
    using with analog cameras, 67
    vs. analog cameras, 4–5
digital converters, 68
digital displays, 86
digital photographs, 95–97. *See also* images;
    photographs
Digital Television (DTV), 12, 14, 86
digital video. *See also* analog video; video
    color and, 29
    converting analog video to, 4–5,
        49–50, 55
    copying to VHS tape, 115
    importing, 55–58
    recording, 7, 70
    shooting tips, 19–41
    size of, 6–7
    storing, 115–116
digital video cameras. *See also* digital
    cameras; video cameras
    accessories. *See* accessories
    aquatic housings, 25
    capacity of, 4
    features, 15–16
    hot-pluggability of, 4, 56
    image sensors, 6, 9, 26
    industrial, 9
    mini-DV, 9
    miniature, 50, 96

one-chip, 9
quality of, 4
resolution, 3
size of, 4
three-chip, 9
two-chip, 9
Digital Video Data Storage (DVDS)
    format, 120
Digital Voodoo Web site, 129
digital zoom feature, 8, 21
direct capture, 67–70
Director's Cut converter, 49
disks. *See* hard disks
distance DV cables, 48
docking stations, 45
dollies, 39
downloading digital photographs, 95–97
drivers
    device drivers, 47
    FireWire drivers, 47, 56
    problems with, 47, 56
    software drivers, 109
    updating, 47
DTV (Digital Television), 12, 14, 86
DV Central Web site, 127
DV clips. *See* clips
DV codec, 7
DV Format Web site, 128
DV Log Pro software, 64
DV Magazine, 128
DV-only capture cards, 46
DV tapes, 5, 8, 115. *See also* videotape
DVCPro50 format, 12
DVD burners, 121
DVD jukebox, 106
DVD-R drives, 121
DVD-R media, 70
DVD-RAM media, 3
DVD recorders, 70

timecode, 63–64
tracks
    audio, 7, 119–120
    subcode, 7
transvideo handheld prompter, 25
tripods, 21, 38, 39
troubleshooting
    chrominance problems, 69
    driver problems, 47, 56
    problems hot-plugging devices, 56
TV. *See* television
TV/FM tuner, 49
two-chip cameras, 9

U

Ultra SCSI interface, 61
ultraviolet light, 22
Umax Astra 6400 printer, 98
Umax Web site, 129
underscanning, 83
Unibrain Web site, 129
USB printers, 98
UV filters, 22

V

VariZoom lens controller, 27
vectorscopes, 67, 68, 69
Vegas Video software, 78, 128
VHS tapes, 116
video. *See also* analog video; digital video
    backups, 58, 107, 110
    black between, 64, 115
    capturing. *See* capturing video
    colorizing, 21
    composite video, 83
    copying to VHS tape, 116
    disk space, 58–59
    importing. *See* importing video
    interlaced, 13, 92

logging footage, 62–66
    motion in, 38
    playback. *See* playback
    preparing for transfer, 117–118
    previewing, 75–76, 83–84
    quality of, 76
    saving, 58
    storing. *See* storage devices
    streaming, 79, 103, 109, 110, 116–117
video area networks, 110–111
video cameras. *See also* analog video
        cameras; digital video cameras
    24P camera, 14
    basic concepts, 6–8
    capturing live video from, 70–72
    connecting to computer, 45
    connecting to tape deck, 46
    connecting to video mixer, 46
    features, 9–14
    handling, 39
    high-definition camcorders, 12–13
    linking, 50
    movement of, 38–39
    one-chip camcorders, 10–11
    previewing video with, 83–84
    price of, 16
    progressive-frame cameras, 13
    status of, 56
    three-chip camcorders, 11–12
video capture cards, 46–47, 68
video CDs, 121
video clips. *See* clips
video compression. *See* compression
Video Finesse plug-in, 68
video mixers, 46
Video Production newsgroup, 127
video signals, 67–68
Video Smith Web site, 127
Video Syncrasies videotape series, 82
video-to-film transfer, 117–118

Videography magazine, 128
Videomaker Magazine, 128
Videonics Web site, 129
VideoRaid RT system, 61
videotape. *See also* DV tapes; video
    archiving, 115–116
    blackstriping, 64, 115
    forwarding, 57
    long-term care, 115
    pausing, 57
    playing. *See* playback
    recording, 57
    rewinding, 57
    speed, 21
    storing offsite, 115
    VHS tapes, 116
viewfinder, 15
vignetting, 23
Vinterberg, Thomas, 10
VST CD-R/W burner, 119
VST RAID Array system, 61
VST Technology Web site, 129

W

waveform monitors, 67, 68, 69
Web. *See also* Internet
    camera movement and, 38–39
    capturing video to, 71–72
    movies for, 79, 116–117, 119
    shooting video for, 33, 51–52
    video for presentation over, 33
    zooming and, 33
Web sites
    Boyce, Bryan, 130
    cameras, 127
    Damaged Californians, 130
    featured filmmakers, 130
    FireWire discussions, 127
    FireWire Filmmaking site, 127